Verdicts & Victories

The Seven Mountains of Culture

Lisa Knight Windahl

Copyright © 2025 Lisa Knight Windahl
All rights reserved.
ISBN: 979-8-9941430-0-1
Imprint: Independently published
Cover by davidmunozart.com

Dedication

To Dr. Thomas Schlueter, a friend, apostolic leader, and trusted co-laborer in the Kingdom.

Your faithfulness, wisdom, and unwavering commitment to Texas and the USA as a covenant land have shaped my journey and sharpened my call. Coauthoring *Analyze and Execute* with you became a defining moment in my life—a prophetic doorway into the writing assignment that unfolds in these pages. Thank you for believing, mentoring, and making room for what God placed within me.

To the intercessors and apostolic leaders of the Texas Apostolic Prayer Network (TXAPN),
my tribe, my family, and my fellow warriors.

You have stood day after day on the walls of this state with courage, discipline, and prophetic clarity. Your labor in hidden places, your steadfast devotion, and your refusal to relent have shaped an atmosphere where the purposes of God can be birthed and established. Thank you for living the call to govern in prayer with integrity and joy.

To Anne Tate and the Whale Riders, a company of seers, watchmen, and spiritual pioneers.
Your sensitivity to the Spirit, your boldness to release what you hear, and your commitment to revelation have strengthened and confirmed my path time and again. Your prophetic insight has carried wind to my sails and weight to my assignments. Thank you for being a watchmen's company that hears, sees, and speaks with purity and precision.

This book is dedicated to each of you.

Your lives, prayers, leadership, and obedience have mattered —more than you know.

You helped shape this work, this mandate, and this moment.

Endorsements

Verdicts & Victories declare the very DNA of the Kingdom of God. It contains prophetic, powerful, practical teachings & tactics in ways that will supercharge the Body of Christ.

Bob Long
Rally Call Min
Austin , TX

When I was first exposed to Lisa Windahl's decrees, I was a bit taken aback. We were being exhorted at a prayer training conference to study them. But how could I, a total novice in "legal-ease" language of the courtroom, ever be able to learn, much less make use of this jargon I found so clumsy in my mouth?

But the Lord stopped me cold when He told me bluntly,"Satan is a legalist!" That's all He said!

I knew He was telling me to explore this new way of speaking to the enemy in a language he knows quite well. The Lord reminded me that the devil is a master at judging, trying, and condemning us by making legal arguments... twisting the Word of God, slandering us to try to stop us cold in our assignments, just as he did Eve in the garden, just as he did Jesus in the wilderness.

And then recently before a prayer strike, the Lord told me, "You must incorporate Lisa's decrees into your arsenal to meet the higher level of warfare today." He said outright to me, "These are 'brilliant strategies' (Prov. 1:5) downloaded from heaven for you to use on this assignment."

I am now so grateful for this marvelous gift, tucked away for decades, being released to the Lord's Ekklesia in the earth "for such a time as this."

Beckie Griffin, Council
Texas Apostolic Prayer Network

When Lisa joined TXAPN, (Texas Apostolic Prayer Network), she immediately shook things up. We understood that we are both Kings and Priests in the order of Melchizedek, as co-heirs with Jesus Christ. However, when Lisa prayed, her decrees seemed to carry a weighted difference. Analyze & Execute, her first book, she explains rules of protocol, jurisdiction, venue, spiritual authority, alignment, divine timing and so much more. All of these are important but listening and obeying the Holy Spirit is key. He guides us and reveals everything we need. She perceived the unusual season the Ekklesia was in and explained, it was the time for us to address the accusations and legal claims with greater authority, accuracy, and precision. This is where we begin establishing territory and grounds in such a way that the enemy cannot appeal or reclaim dominion. Our legal standing for this is Isaiah 35:8

God has given Lisa many gifts and talents. She embodies a sharp legal mind and was born to write. I see that she is anointed, to shift and shape the understanding of the legal rights we possess.

Thanks be to God for her and the other praise filled warriors we serve with. God continues to develop strong covenant relationships within the Body of Christ. If you haven't found yours, open up your home and invite one person to pray, or join others who are already gathering. We have the honor of listening to our Fathers voice and then to strike the mark!

Jill Muzechenko
President, 32 99 Harvest Hub, Abilene, TX.
Rolling Plains Director w/ TXAPN (Texas Apostolic Prayer Network) Texas
General w/ RPN (Reformation Prayer Network)

Spend a short time with Lisa Knight Windahl and you quickly recognize that her love for the Lord fuels every word and action she offers; her devotion echoes the psalmist who delights in the Lord and is renewed (Psalm 37:4). Her hunger for the Kingdom and for Yahusha Hamachi is evident in both conversation and counsel, for she seeks first the Kingdom and its righteousness (Matthew 6:33).

The imprint of this devotion is unmistakable in the book she co-authored, Analyze and Execute: God's Strategy for the Ekklesia to Govern, where biblical clarity and practical governance intersect. To encounter Lisa is to meet someone who lives by the Word that became flesh and dwelt among us, bearing truth that transforms lives (John 1:14).

I was especially drawn to her Verdicts & Victories Volume One because it harmonized with revelations I have received from the Holy Spirit and introduced fresh insights that deepened my faith (Revelation 12:11). Every chapter reads like a testimony of one who does not merely teach about the power of prayer, decrees, and proclamations, but walks in their effectiveness, demonstrating that faith is active and persevering (James 2:17). I wholeheartedly recommend Verdicts & Victories Volume One to those who hunger for kingdom substance; within its pages you will find treasures that lead not only to understanding but to tangible liberation in Christ (John 8:32)

Dr. Russell Welch
Senior Pastor Highway to Heaven Church
Co-Founder, Remnant Warrior Ministries
Warrior's Discipleship School

Verdicts and Victories is Power Packed, but it's dangerous to read as you will never be the same intercessor you were. These 54 pages of Truth that will, when implemented, set America and this world FREE! You will never fight in intercession with lessor weapons as Lisa has handed you Holy Spirit Bombs! I'm amazing how Holy Spirit has dictated to Lisa a Spiritual Warfare Manual that summons His people to our NOW season-changing us from <u>no longer praying save passive precatory prayers</u> by (asking God, pleading with God, begging God to fix everything in this world that's broken, while we walk away saying, if God wants this fixed, He will do it; if not, He won't – WRONG!) to <u>confident warriors decreeing His word.</u> You can never walk away from a spiritual fight against and you won't want to, for our fights are "rigged rights" as Jesus has already won every battle! We are called to war, to decree each battles predetermined WIN. This manual educates, elevates, empowers, commissions any novice or mature intercessor, to a new, exciting level of warfare prayer. In only 54 pages what has taken many of us decades to learn and to practice, you are blessed to receive NOW.

Why is warfare Prayer exciting you may ask – because it changes what is now to what God's original intention for our world has always been, but was lost or stolen; you pray His heart, so there's no wondering if what you are praying is God's will and intent. This manual removes the question: do I have His authority to announce these Decrees. YES you do! Jesus shed His blood for us to be given His authority. He died, arose from the dead, ascended into heaven and sat down at the right hand of God – when He said **it is finished**, it was! Then Jesus handed ALL of His authority over to us His intercessors-us!

Jesus accomplished what He was born for, now we are to do the same!

He is waiting on us to arise from being Christian spectators to become Powerful Participants – launching His decrees into our atmosphere, into all 7 mountains of culture and influence from their top to their bottom. In doing this, we are shifting unrighteous anti-God assignments that have been levied against His people, His world, by His enemies causing them to cease, desist and have no further effect! WooHoo, no we are getting somewhere!

This manual solidifies who we are and are not. Whose we are. Why He has need of us to decree with authority to nullify the enemy's works. How to fulfill our mighty work of Jeremiah 1:10 – *I have appointed you to the oversight of the nations and of the Kings to root out, to pull down, and to destroy and to overthrow, to build and to plant,* thus bringing into being God's original purpose for His world and His intercessors to be brought to the forefront. We are NO LONGER back-row people, not passive, not complacent, not expecting God or the leaders of The Body to be the only ones to move mountains!

These 54 pages hand us intercessors the tools to "call what is not as though it were and it shall become that which was decreed, It shall come to pass!"

There's no fear here, beloved.

ENJOY & TAKE NO CAPTIVES

Suzanne Harrington
TXAPN Council
SPAN, Glory of Zion Elder
NEI
Josiah Company

Lisa Windahl has written more than a book in Verdicts and Victories. She has perfectly interpreted the times in which we are living and pressing out new and higher revelation during these PEY years. This decade we are joining with the focus of the Lord as He invites us higher to overcome our enemies and frame our future as He makes His will known to us and His directions for us by using our voice to speak.

Lisa is a true Watchman and she is mobilizing and activating others to pourout direct heavenly responses into chaotic situations created by the spirit of this age to cause fear and dread in God's people. We are seeing situations change and freedom won by concentrating on listening for the Lord and speaking what He says rather than reacting out of our own emotions or opinions.
She has modeled connecting with the Spirit of the word.

The Whale Riders have tested these words and decrees, we have released them with her and in the process received greater revelation and more intense connection with the Lord and the pulling down of His kingdom on earth as it is in heaven.

We are living in some very exciting times where the Lord is giving us incredible strategies to overcome and to birth forth all that He would bless this nation and the nations of the earth with. We will not fulfill what we are being called to execute if we do not use these years to vav with our mouth the new administration that is coming down.

We will not disrupt the plans of our enemies to steal, kill and destroy unless we allow ourselves to Rise and Shine as His light comes. This book is filled with His light!

Anne S Tate
International Director of Prayer and the Watches
Glory of Zion, International
Apostolic Watchman
Founder of Whale Riders – Global Watchmen Call

Verdicts and Victories is a lifeline for every believer willing to take their place in the Kingdom of God. The pages are filled with ammunition and strategies for the Ekklesia to hit their mark and destroy the works of the enemy. This resource is not just for high-level intercessors; the power of the Holy Spirit empowers and activates everyone's calling in their respective assignments in The Seven Mountains of Culture.

I am immensely grateful for Lisa's life. Her hands have been trained for battle through her personal experiences, leading to writings that make hell tremble. I was divinely introduced to her by the Holy Spirit during the 5786 Head of the Year Conference at Glory of Zion Ministries in Corinth, Texas. Since then, my life as a mother and business intercessor has skyrocketed, thanks to the confidence her writings—filled with heavenly downloads—have inspired in me.

Her work provides divine strategies to demolish strongholds that need to be addressed in my bloodline and place of business. The fight for our families, our faith, the education of future generations, our government, our economy, and the media and arts is one that every believer must engage in. This is a God-given armory to accomplish that mission. The gates of hell will not prevail against the Ekklesia of Christ.

Leonor B Interiano
Family and Business Intercessor
Intercessors for America

Lisa, in her book, Verdicts and Victories, has knocked it out of the park. When I was first introduced to Lisa and the declarations that God put upon her heart to pen, I saw a gifting there that really struck my heart deeply. But this book, as I've read over the manuscript, as I've pressed into it, I want you to know this is an absolute essential resource that we need for the time that we're in. So, I ask you to buy this book, and as you read this book, do so with that in your mind. Also buy it so it can be a gift to someone else.

This book is filled with not just revelation, but it's filled with spiritual understanding, and the declarations are so strong.
Thank you, Lisa, for your dedication to this book. Thank you for the book that is just so significant at this time. And yes, it's time for us to move into Verdicts and Victories, and thank you for penning this book, putting words on these pages that will cause people to excel in their ability to make declarations which will cause the Ekklesia to stand out in this new era we've moved into. God bless you for writing this book.

Clay Nash
Clay Nash Ministries
Author of:
Activating the Prophetic
Relational Authority Authentic Leadership
God Dreams to Make America Great Again
Aligned for Conquest

Foreword

"In the last days, the mountain of Yahweh's temple, will be raised up as the head of the mountains, towering over all the hills. A sparkling stream of every nation will flow into it" (Isaiah 2:2 The Passion Translation).

I vividly remember a sermon that I was about to preach over twenty years ago. The topic was going to be the Seven Mountains of Culture. Most of us are familiar with the teaching that goes back to the revelations that Lauren Cunningham and Bill Bright had many years ago. Over the years there have been many commentaries, books, dialogues, and teachings regarding the seven mountains. So, I jumped in because the water was fine.

I had my sermon ready, and I was about ready to open up my message when the Lord spoke to me and declared. You will not preach that this morning. There's nothing like a divine interruption in the midst of a sermon being decreed or declared, that causes one to become very fearful of number one, what was God was referring to and two, fearful of not giving a message to my congregation that morning. I needed a quick answer to the next question. What Lord is it that you want me to preach?

The context of my message that morning on the Seven mountains was going to declare that the religion mountain, which most people presume to be the Church, would be the influencer of all the rest of the six mountains, causing God's reformation and transformation to take place in the earth. But the Lord made it very clear to me that day that if you have the religion mountain influencing the other six mountains, you now have an overbearing religious spirit being present over all the rest of culture. That is not God's intent or design.

Then the Lord opened up my eyes, and I saw in my spirit the mountain of the Lord. It soared above all the mountains of culture. And He revealed to me that from this mountain, He will send forth His church, His Ekklesia, to influence all of culture. What an amazing revelation.

And now you have in your hands a book, **Verdicts and Victories**, by my friend Lisa Knight Windahl that takes us even deeper into what needs to be decreed and declared over these seven mountains from the mountain of the Lord. We can't just teach about this. We can't just analyze it. You can read about analyzing in the book that we wrote together – Analyze and Execute. God is expecting us to rise up with His authority that He has granted each of us. We are seated with Him in the heavenly places. We are in the third heaven with Him. And He has given us full authority to decree, to execute, and to bring about the verdicts that need to be rendered on earth as it is in heaven.

When I first met Lisa, I was overwhelmed by the Lord's revelations that she had been given to release decrees and declarations via the power of the Holy Spirit. These decrees were not manufactured out of human reasoning but released by the Spirit as tools of executing God's will on earth. Her training and vocation as a paralegal gives her a unique God-given ability to render the decrees and verdicts as legal renderings.
Just weeks after our book, Analyze and Execute, was published, the Lord brought another revelation to me based on Isaiah 33:22.

"The Lord Yahweh is our judge, our lawgiver, and our king; He will save us completely" (Isaiah 33:22 The Passion Translation).

The Lord then went on to reveal a truth that I already knew. Our government in Washington, D.C. is formulated on these three principles. The three branches of our government are the executive, the legislative, and the judicial. He then went on to decree, "It's the same structure that I have given my Ekklesia to govern." We have moved into a very powerful season of understanding the ultimate authority that God has given us in order to write executive decrees, carry out legislative orders, and render judgments regarding what He needs to release from heaven into the atmosphere of the earth and especially into our nation, into our states, and yes, even into our personal lives. Lisa has been given a great gift in this hour to hear the Spirit as He releases verdicts from heaven. These verdicts and decrees that need to be made in order to reform and transform our nation.

Let's make something clear. The Lord is not developing a theocracy where He will now become the seat of government that is held by the President of the United States. That's far below his pay grade. But He is desiring and exhorting each of us to be those that would influence not just government, but all of the mountains of culture with the influence of His wisdom, His revelations, His strategies, His verdicts, and His decrees.

Lisa is an instrument that the Lord is using right now to procure verdicts and decrees that are filtered through her trained occupation as a paralegal. She is bringing those decrees, declarations, and verdicts into clear focus as we render them as members of the Ekklesia.

Well done, Lisa. Let me close with one last thought. Lisa and I have talked about this at great length. These **Verdicts and Victories** are not meant to be an easy way out of doing something that the Lord has commanded all of us to be a part of. We pray that these decrees, strategies, verdicts, and teachings will ignite each one of you to personally go into the throne room of God and to ask him, "Lord, what is that you would have me decree."

Dr. Thomas Schlueter
KingdomGate, Arlington, Texas – Apostle
Texas Apostolic Prayer Network, Apostle and Coordinator

Preface

The days we are living in are marked by upheaval, acceleration, and unprecedented spiritual conflict. Yet they are also marked by prophetic clarity and divine opportunity. The Ekklesia is being summoned into its original identity—not as an audience, but as a governing assembly; not as a passive church, but as Heaven's legislative body.

This book, *Verdicts and Victories*, emerges from years of spiritual assignments, courtroom encounters, prophetic intelligence, and legislative decrees. It builds upon foundations laid in earlier work, including *Analyze and Execute*—a manual that has already served as a catalytic resource for high-level intercessors and apostolic leaders across the nation.[1] The endorsements that accompanied *Analyze and Execute* confirm its significance, including the powerful affirmation from Don Crum of Leadership International and Project Bridgestone, who described it as a "weapons-grade… warfare manual" essential for the Ekklesia in this hour.[2]

As history continues to unfold at a rapid pace, the Lord is requiring His people to function with precision, legal standing, and governmental authority. This volume provides the essential framework for understanding jurisdiction, venue, standing, timing, unity, legal language, and enforcement. Every decree you will find in the pages ahead has been written with the same spiritual jurisprudence that shaped *Analyze and Execute*—but this book expands the operating

---

[1] Analyze and Execute, God's Strategy for the Ekklesia to Govern, Schlueter & Windahl.

[2] Analyze and Execute, Don Crum endorsement, Leadership International / Project Bridgestone, Washington, D.C.

scope to the Seven Mountains of Culture, where spiritual rulership must now manifest with clarity and boldness.

It is my conviction that the Ekklesia is entering its most significant era since the book of Acts. The days of passive Christianity have expired. These are days of governmental Christianity—days of verdicts issued, victories secured, and Kingdom rule enforced. This book is written for those ready to legislate Heaven's justice into the earth with precision, faith, and holy boldness.

It is impossible to rightly govern a world without God and without the Scriptures. That truth—often attributed to George Washington—frames the mandate of this work: to reintroduce the Ekklesia to its judicial and governmental identity.

The Ekklesia is God's ruling council in the earth. It is His embassy, His court, His legislative assembly. Christ, the Head of the Church, declared that *all* authority in Heaven and on earth belongs to Him, and He entrusts that authority to His Body so that His will can be established in every sphere of culture. The Church is not peripheral to the world; the world is peripheral to the Church.

When the Ekklesia rises in its governmental function—praying, decreeing, binding, loosing, and legislating from Heaven's perspective—territories shift, cultures reform, and demonic systems collapse. The apostolic church of Acts understood this. Heaven backed them because they legislated rather than spectated. They prayed united, spoke united, and acted united—and everything around them shook.

Verdicts and Victories builds upon the principles of strategic analysis and execution that were introduced in *Analyze and Execute*—principles that have now become essential for every believer operating in the courts of Heaven. The Ekklesia must learn not only to intercede but to govern; not only to discern but to decree; not only to ask but to execute.

This book will guide you into that dimension of Kingdom responsibility. Each section addresses a critical cultural mountain—Religion, Family, Education, Government, Media, Arts & Entertainment, and Business & Economy—providing scriptural authority and actionable decrees that position the Ekklesia to legislate righteousness into these systems.

We stand at a defining moment. The nations are in upheaval, but Heaven is not. The King is issuing verdicts, and the Ekklesia is being summoned to enforce them. The world is waiting—not for another sermon—but for a governing church.

This book is the fruit of a call that Heaven released long before my hands began to write it. Over the course of months, the Lord used His prophets, His servants, and His own voice to confirm a singular mandate: *Write.*

Again and again, the word of the Lord came—sometimes as a whisper, sometimes as fire—declaring that writing would not simply be an assignment, but a mantle, a responsibility tied to governance, intercession, and the destiny of nations.

Holy Spirit impressed upon my heart that the assignment would come forth with a timing and magnitude beyond my expectations. Others began to see what I had not yet fully embraced—books, manuals, blueprints, and resources that would be more than teaching.

They would be instruments of Kingdom administration. Tools for the Ekklesia. Weapons for intercession. Strategies that prevent war, activate watchmen, and train the next generation.

This call to write did not come in isolation. It built upon a pattern the Lord had already established in my life. One of the early confirmations came through the book *Analyze and Execute*, which I coauthored with Dr. Thomas Schlueter. That project became a foundational training ground—an introduction to stewarding revelation, discerning spiritual intelligence, and converting insight into action. It served as a forerunner to this work, sharpening the scribe-warrior mantle that the Lord would later confirm through prophetic words and repeated instructions to write.

Through numerous prophetic confirmations, it became clear that writing was a central component of my calling, and that multiple works would emerge from that assignment. They spoke of a scribe-anointing, of heavenly blueprints, and of a divine library where I would receive what must be written *line by line, precept upon precept.*

They described a season when the Lord Himself would pour into me so that I could pour out again—fresh fire, fresh oil, and a mantle to ignite others. They saw what I did not yet see: that writing would become one of the primary vehicles through which the Lord would extend His justice, His fire, and His governance into the earth.

In these words, the Lord also confirmed that the Ekklesia is transitioning from wildfire starters to firestorm igniters—and that the writings birthed in this season would carry that same firestorm assignment. I was told that these books would help bring the Ekklesia into its role as a ruling body, a governing people who legislate through decree, prayer, and righteous authority.

What began as scattered embers has now become a culmination of fire-filled revelation—pages ignited by the breath of the Spirit, fueled by prophetic commissioning, and anchored in biblical truth.

Verdicts and Victories is not simply a book. It is part of the assignment spoken over me: to write what Heaven is releasing so the Ekklesia can rise into its rightful mandate. It is one expression of the firestorm the Lord is forming across His people—decrees, resolutions, strategies, and instructions that align with His justice, His Kingdom, and His victory.

This preface marks the fulfillment of the prophetic words that declared I would write… and write… and keep writing. It is the doorway into a work that carries the fingerprints of the Father, the fire of the Spirit, and the commissioning of Heaven. May these pages equip you, ignite you, and position you to legislate with clarity, authority, and confidence as part of the ruling Ekklesia of Jesus Christ.

This is the season of fire. This is the season of enforcement of heaven's verdicts. This is the season of victories.

And this is only the beginning.

TABLE OF CONTENTS

INTRODUCTION — 25

ARTS & ENTERTAINMENT — 53

BUSINESS AND ECONOMY MOUNTAIN — 61

EDUCATION MOUNTAIN — 69

FAMILY MOUNTAIN — 77

GOVERNMENT MOUNTAIN — 87

MEDIA MOUNTAIN — 97

RELIGION MOUNTAIN — 105

ABOUT THE AUTHOR — 115

OTHER BOOKS BY THE AUTHOR — 117

INTRODUCTION

"It is impossible to rightly govern the world without God and the Bible."
— *Attributed to George Washington*

THE RULING AUTHORITY OF THE EKKLESIA AND ITS MANDATE OVER THE SEVEN MOUNTAINS

The Ekklesia is God's instrument of Kingdom administration in the earth. It is His embassy, His legislative body, and His court of decree. The authority of the Ekklesia does not originate in human systems but in divine covenant. Christ, the Head of the Church, has *"all authority in Heaven and on earth"* (Matthew 28:18), and He delegates that authority to His body to enforce His rule. The Church is therefore not peripheral to the world; the world is peripheral to the Church (Ephesians 1:22–23 MSG).

When the Ekklesia rises in governmental function—praying, decreeing, and legislating from Heaven's perspective—territories shift, cultures reform, and justice is established. The Ekklesia is the restraining and reforming force in the earth (2 Thessalonians 2:6–7), designed to occupy until He comes (Luke 19:13). Through prophetic decrees, courtroom petitions, and spiritual legislation, the sons and daughters of God advance the dominion of Christ until *"the kingdoms of this world have become the Kingdoms of our Lord and of His Christ"* (Revelation 11:15).

From the beginning, God ordained the earth to be governed by His sons and daughters in covenant partnership with Him (Genesis 1:26–28; Psalm 8:4–6). Dominion was never meant to be exercised through human ambition but through divine representation by those made in His image who carry His Spirit, His wisdom, and His authority. When Jesus declared, *"I will build My Ekklesia, and the gates of Hades shall not prevail against it"* (Matthew 16:18), He restored Heaven's original governmental intent, which is a ruling body of believers called to execute the decrees of the King and enforce the victory of the Cross in every sphere of creation (Colossians 2:15).

The Ekklesia is not merely a congregation or religious institution. It is Heaven's governmental assembly on earth. The Greek term *ekklesia* refers to a legislative body of citizens summoned to deliberate, decree, and govern on behalf of the ruling power. Jesus appropriated this governmental term intentionally, defining His Church as a spiritual parliament endowed with Kingdom authority. To this body, He gave *"the keys of the Kingdom of Heaven"* (Matthew 16:19) symbolic of legal access, jurisdiction, and the right to legislate Heaven's will upon the earth.

The Ekklesia is therefore the extension of Christ's government into time and history. As those who have been *"raised up together and seated with Him in the heavenly places"* (Ephesians 2:6), the sons and daughters of God legislate from the finished position of Christ's victory, declaring His decrees into the structures of the earth. Through this divine partnership, Heaven's will is executed through human agency, fulfilling the prayer of Jesus: *"Your Kingdom come, Your will be done on earth as it is in Heaven"* (Matthew 6:10).

The Ekklesia operates as a judicial body in the spirit realm. It hears Heaven's verdicts, discerns divine rulings, and releases them through decrees and intercession. When the Ekklesia speaks in alignment with the King, its decrees carry judicial force and legislative impact. Heaven backs the word of its ambassadors (2 Corinthians 5:20), angels are dispatched (Psalm 103:20), and demonic thrones are displaced.

This is not mere symbolism. Scripture affirms that the saints *"shall judge the world"* and *"shall judge angels"* (1 Corinthians 6:2–3), revealing the magnitude of delegated authority entrusted to the redeemed. The Ekklesia therefore does not react to darkness - it governs over it. From its heavenly seat, it issues divine verdicts that shape history, establish justice, and realign territories under the Kingship of Christ (Psalm 149:5–9).

Because the Kingdom of God encompasses every aspect of life, the jurisdiction of the Ekklesia extends into all Seven Mountains of Culture, the arenas of dominion that mold the thought, behavior, and destiny of nations: Religion, Family, Education, Government, Media, Arts & Entertainment, and Economy. These spheres are the modern "high places" where altars of worship, ideology, and influence are erected. Whichever spirit governs these mountains governs the moral and prophetic direction of society (Deuteronomy 12:2–3; 2 Kings 17:9–12).

1. **The Mountain of Religion** must be cleansed of idolatry, corruption, and human traditions that obscure

the revelation of Christ. It must once again become the fountain of truth and worship in spirit and in truth (John 4:23–24; Isaiah 56:7).

Among the Seven Mountains, the Mountain of Religion is the most contested, for it concerns the very seat of spiritual allegiance and worship on the earth. Yet the Kingdom of God was never intended to be a religion - it is the government of the Most High manifested through His sons and daughters in covenant authority. Religion is man's attempt to reach God; the Kingdom is God's government invading the realm of man.

The Ekklesia stands as Heaven's ruling body within this sphere. It does not exist to compete among faiths or enforce human belief systems, but to demonstrate and administrate the supremacy of the One True God - YHWH, the Most High - whose Kingdom rules over all (Psalm 103:19). The Ekklesia functions as the embassy of that government, carrying spiritual authority that transcends denominational lines and religious traditions. Its role is to restore the earth's spiritual order to divine alignment, confronting idolatry, syncretism, and deception with the revelation of the risen Christ.

Where religion builds systems, the Ekklesia builds altars of presence. Where religion controls through fear, the Ekklesia governs through love and truth. It is written, "The hour is coming, and now is, when the true worshipers will worship the Father in spirit and truth" (John 4:23). True worship is governmental - it enthrones the Lord in the midst of His people (Psalm 22:3) and displaces every false god and counterfeit throne.

The Ekklesia is therefore Heaven's authorized power within the spiritual dimension of nations. Through decree, prayer, and prophetic legislation, it reclaims the sacred spaces that religion defiled and re-establishes the dominion of the Most High. It does not coerce conscience but governs atmosphere - subduing principalities and establishing environments where the Spirit of Truth reigns unhindered. As Elijah confronted Baal (1 Kings 18:21–39) and Moses confronted Pharaoh's magicians (Exodus 7–12), so the modern Ekklesia confronts spiritual counterfeit systems, declaring, "The Lord, He is God!"

This mountain is not merely about temples, churches, or doctrines; it is about spiritual jurisdiction. Whoever occupies this mountain determines which spirit governs the moral and prophetic tone of a nation. For too long, religious confusion and compromise have occupied it, enthroning tradition above revelation. The Ekklesia is rising to displace those thrones, to release the pure river of the Spirit once again into the nations (Revelation 22:1–2).

Our mandate is not to promote "Christian religion" as one among many, but to manifest the unshakable Kingdom of God (Hebrews 12:28), a government of righteousness, peace, and joy in the Holy Spirit (Romans 14:17). The Ekklesia stands as the ruling priesthood of that Kingdom, ministering before the Lord, legislating His decrees, and extending His dominion throughout the earth (1 Peter 2:9; Revelation 1:6).

In this era, the Mountain of Religion must bow to the government of the Lamb. The idols of human reason, ritual, and rebellion will fall, and the knowledge of the glory of the Lord will fill every temple, house, and heart (Habakkuk 2:14). The Ekklesia will not serve religion, it will reign with the King, revealing His presence, enforcing His rule, and restoring true spiritual authority to the nations.

2. **The Mountain of Family** is the cornerstone of society, reflecting the covenantal nature of the Father. It must be restored to divine order—where fathers lead, mothers nurture, and children are trained in the ways of the Lord (Genesis 18:19; Ephesians 5:22–33; 6:1–4).

The Mountain of Family is the cornerstone of every society and the primary structure through which the nature of the Father is revealed in the earth. Before there was a nation, a priesthood, or a church, there was a family. The divine order of the family was established in Eden, where man and woman, made in the image of God, were joined in covenant to steward creation and multiply godly seed (Genesis 1:26–28; 2:18–24). This original design was not merely biological or social, it was governmental and covenantal. The family was created as the first expression of dominion and discipleship, a microcosm of Heaven's order operating in the earth.

When sin entered, that divine structure was fractured. The serpent did not attack the garden, he attacked the marriage, knowing that if he could corrupt the covenant, he could corrupt the generations. To this day, the Mountain of Family remains one of the most fiercely contested battlefields in the spirit realm, because whoever shapes the family shapes the future. Every culture's strength or collapse can be traced to how it honors or distorts God's order for the home.

In God's design, the family reveals His nature and government. The Fatherhood of God is mirrored through righteous earthly fathers who lead with integrity, love, and strength (Ephesians 3:14–15). Mothers reflect the nurturing heart and wisdom of the

Spirit (Proverbs 31:10–31). Together, they form a covenantal unit that imparts identity, inheritance, and discipline to their children (Deuteronomy 6:6–9; Proverbs 22:6). Children, raised in the fear of the Lord, become carriers of legacy - arrows released into destiny (Psalm 127:3–5).

The war against family is ultimately a war against divine order, manifested through fatherlessness, gender confusion, generational rebellion, and the redefinition of covenant. These are not merely social issues, they are spiritual strategies designed to dismantle the reflection of God's nature in human form. Where the family breaks down, authority collapses, and nations lose their moral compass (Malachi 4:5–6).

Therefore, the Ekklesia must rise as a prophetic and judicial voice to rebuild the ancient foundations (Isaiah 58:12). We are called to decree divine alignment, to defend the sanctity of marriage, and to restore the covenantal bond between parents and children. Fathers must return to their posts as protectors, providers, and priests of their homes. Mothers must be honored as wise builders and nurturers of destiny. The generations must be reconciled so that blessing replaces curse and legacy replaces loss (Malachi 4:6).

The Mountain of Family is also where Kingdom multiplication begins. Revival that does not reform the family cannot sustain transformation. The Ekklesia's goal is not only to build churches but to raise households of faith—families that carry the culture of the Kingdom into every sphere of society. Each covenant home becomes an embassy of Heaven, a governmental outpost where love, truth, and authority flow from the presence of God. When homes are aligned under divine government, entire communities and nations are stabilized under righteousness (Joshua 24:15; Psalm 112:1–2).

The restoration of this mountain requires both spiritual warfare and cultural reformation. The Ekklesia must confront demonic ideologies that assault identity, pervert sexuality, and destroy covenant. We must legislate from Heaven that every counterfeit definition of marriage and family be exposed and overturned. We must decree the return of fathers to their children, mothers to their assignments, and sons and daughters to their purpose. When the family is healed, the nation is healed; when the covenant order of the home is restored, the dominion of Christ expands through generations.

The Mountain of Family is not simply about domestic life, it is about government, legacy, and continuity of Kingdom authority. Therefore, the Ekklesia must guard this mountain with vigilance and wisdom, legislating restoration until every home becomes a reflection of the Father's house, filled with light, truth, and the glory of the Most High.

2. **The Mountain of Education** shapes the minds of generations. It must be redeemed to teach wisdom rooted in the fear of the Lord (Proverbs 9:10), displacing doctrines of deception with truth and understanding.

    The Mountain of Education governs the formation of thought, belief, and identity in every society. It is the system through which values are transmitted, ideologies are established, and worldviews are shaped. Whoever controls education controls the future, for it is through the shaping of minds that nations are steered toward either righteousness or rebellion. This mountain determines not only what a generation *knows*, but *who* they become.

In its original design, education was never secular—it was sacred. Instruction flowed from the revelation of God's wisdom. The fear of the Lord was the foundation of all knowledge (Proverbs 9:10), and learning was viewed as a form of worship, cultivating both intellect and character to reflect divine truth. The Hebrew word for "teach" (*lamad*) implies not just transferring information, but imparting understanding that leads to transformation. God intended education to produce wise rulers, righteous leaders, and covenant-keeping families who would carry His ways to the next generation (Deuteronomy 6:6–9; Psalm 78:4–7).

But when the spirit of Babylon infiltrated the educational systems of the world, truth was replaced with humanism, relativism, and deception. The modern system, once meant to reveal the Creator, now seeks to erase Him. Classrooms have become battlegrounds for ideology rather than altars of wisdom. Children are indoctrinated in godlessness under the banner of "progress," and universities have become temples of intellectual pride rather than houses of truth. As in Daniel's day, Babylon still seeks to rename, reprogram, and repurpose the next generation, disconnecting them from covenant identity and divine purpose (Daniel 1:3–7).

The Ekklesia, as Heaven's governing body, carries the mandate to confront and redeem this mountain. The battle for education is not merely academic, it is spiritual and governmental. The spirit of deception seeks to occupy the gates of learning so it can control the language, logic, and laws of the future. But the Ekklesia holds the keys of wisdom and understanding, entrusted by the Spirit of Truth (John 16:13). We are called to decree that education be restored to its rightful purpose: to reveal the glory, order, and wisdom of the Most High.

To redeem the Mountain of Education, the Ekklesia must legislate for truth to displace deception. False doctrines must be exposed, corrupted curricula must be uprooted, and educators must be reawakened to the sacred responsibility of shaping minds in righteousness. The Ekklesia must also raise up righteous reformers, like teachers, professors, administrators, and innovators, anointed to rebuild the walls of learning according to the pattern of Heaven (Isaiah 58:12; Nehemiah 2:18).

Education must once again teach that truth is absolute, that wisdom begins with reverence, and that every field of knowledge points back to its Creator (Colossians 1:16–17). Mathematics reveals divine order, science unveils His power, language reflects His Word, and history records His dealings with humanity. To know truth apart from God is to know confusion and to know God is to understand all things rightly (Proverbs 2:6).

The Ekklesia's role is to open ancient wells of revelation and to restore the biblical model of teaching where the Spirit of wisdom and understanding reigns (Isaiah 11:2). Through decrees and spiritual legislation, the Ekklesia establishes divine protection over the minds of children and youth, breaking the strongholds of indoctrination and identity confusion. We declare that the next generation will not be conformed to this world but transformed by the renewing of their minds (Romans 12:2).

The reformation of this mountain begins wherever truth is enthroned, whether in classrooms, homeschool tables, online platforms, or Kingdom academies. The Ekklesia must occupy every educational gate with prophetic discernment and apostolic authority, ensuring that the light of revelation dispels every shadow of falsehood. When the Spirit of Truth governs the gates of education, nations will produce leaders who walk in wisdom, justice, and divine understanding.

The Mountain of Education must no longer be ruled by the philosophies of men but by the wisdom of the Most High. The Ekklesia legislates this reformation until every school, university, and institution of learning aligns with Heaven's truth, and the knowledge of the Lord covers the earth as the waters cover the sea (Habakkuk 2:14).

2. **The Mountain of Government** must align with justice and righteousness, which are the foundation of God's throne (Psalm 89:14; Isaiah 9:6–7). Civil authority is ordained to serve divine order, not human tyranny (Romans 13:1–4).

   The Mountain of Government is the sphere of authority that shapes laws, policies, and the administration of justice within a nation. It determines how power is exercised, how order is maintained, and how righteousness is upheld in the public domain. Scripture reveals that *"righteousness and justice are the foundation of His throne"* (Psalm 89:14), meaning that every expression of true government must mirror the nature of God's own rule. Civil authority was never intended to replace divine authority—it was designed to reflect it.

   From the beginning, governance was a divine concept. The first governmental command given to humanity was the commission to "subdue and have dominion" (Genesis 1:28). Dominion was not tyranny but stewardship under divine order. When mankind rebelled against God's law, human government became corrupted by pride, greed, and idolatry, producing oppression instead of justice. Yet God never relinquished His design. He anointed righteous rulers to demonstrate His standard - Joseph in Egypt, Moses in Israel, David in Jerusalem, and Daniel in Babylon - each serving as a prophetic model of Heaven's rule on earth.

Isaiah prophesied of Christ, the ultimate King, saying, *"The government shall be upon His shoulders... of the increase of His government and peace there shall be no end"* (Isaiah 9:6–7). This eternal Kingdom government now functions through His Body, the Ekklesia, which has been commissioned to represent His authority within the nations. The Ekklesia does not merely pray for governments, it legislates with Heaven's authority to ensure that civil power aligns with divine order. When earthly thrones rebel against righteousness, the Ekklesia petitions the Court of Heaven and decrees justice from the higher seat of authority (Psalm 97:2; Daniel 7:27).

The purpose of government, according to Scripture, is to uphold good and restrain evil (Romans 13:1–4). When rulers operate under the fear of the Lord, nations prosper and peace prevails (Proverbs 29:2). But when governments exalt human will above divine law, they cross into rebellion, becoming instruments of tyranny rather than servants of justice. Throughout history, God has raised up prophetic reformers to confront unrighteous authority—Moses before Pharaoh, Elijah before Ahab, Nathan before David, John the Baptist before Herod. In every generation, Heaven calls forth the Ekklesia to stand in that same spirit of truth, declaring, *"The Most High rules in the kingdom of men and gives it to whomever He wills"* (Daniel 4:17).

The Ekklesia's governmental mandate is twofold: to pray and to legislate. Prayer invokes Heaven's counsel and legislation enforces Heaven's verdict. Together, they form the spiritual architecture through which nations are aligned with divine justice. Through prophetic decrees, courtroom petitions, and intercessory governance, the Ekklesia binds the powers of corruption, dethrones wicked rulers, and establishes righteous leadership in the gates of nations. It decrees that every law contrary to divine order be overturned and that the counsel of the Lord stand as the supreme authority (Proverbs 19:21).

Government is not inherently political, it is spiritual at its root. Every system of authority is ultimately an altar to one kingdom or another. Either it serves the Kingdom of Light or it perpetuates the dominion of darkness. The Ekklesia is Heaven's counter-government within the earth, authorized to confront corruption, to legislate righteousness, and to install leaders who honor the fear of the Lord. This is not done by carnal power or human manipulation, but by spiritual jurisdiction and prophetic decree (Zechariah 4:6).

The United States' founders recognized this spiritual reality when George Washington observed that *"it is impossible to rightly govern the world without God and the Bible."* Though this phrase is often paraphrased, it echoes his conviction expressed in the Farewell Address (1796):

> *"Of all the dispositions and habits which lead to political prosperity, religion and morality are indispensable supports... Reason and experience both forbid us to expect that*

national morality can prevail in exclusion of religious principle."

Such understanding reflects the Kingdom truth that no nation can long endure apart from divine moral law. The Ekklesia stands as the guardian of that law—Heaven's watchtower over the affairs of men—declaring that governments must once again bow to the government of God.

As the Ekklesia legislates from its seated position in Christ (Ephesians 2:6), it releases decrees that dismantle the thrones of corruption, expose deception, and install righteous leadership across cities, states, and nations. It declares that unjust laws will not stand, that systems built on lies will crumble, and that the foundation of justice and righteousness will be restored under the lordship of Christ. For *"the kingdoms of this world shall become the kingdoms of our Lord and of His Christ, and He shall reign forever and ever"* (Revelation 11:15).

The Mountain of Government is therefore the visible expression of spiritual authority in a nation. As the Ekklesia rises in her full governmental identity, she will transform this mountain from a seat of corruption into a throne of righteousness. The fear of the Lord will once again be the beginning of policy, truth will return to the halls of justice, and civil authority will serve divine order instead of human ambition. When this happens, nations will find their true peace—not in the will of man, but in the rule of the Most High.

3. **The Mountain of Media** wields immense power to frame perception and narrative. It must be purified from falsehood, manipulation, and censorship, becoming a channel of truth and light (Ephesians 4:25; Psalm 15:2–3).

The Mountain of Government is therefore the visible expression of spiritual authority in a nation. As the Ekklesia rises in her full governmental identity, she will transform this mountain from a seat of corruption into a throne of righteousness. The fear of the Lord will once again be the beginning of policy, truth will return to the halls of justice, and civil authority will serve divine order instead of human ambition. When this happens, nations will find their true peace—not in the will of man, but in the rule of the Most High.

The Mountain of Media is one of the most influential and volatile arenas of power in the modern world. It governs perception, frames reality, and steers the consciousness of nations. Through the flow of information - spoken, written, and broadcast - beliefs are shaped, emotions are stirred, and societal direction is determined. Words can build or destroy, heal or wound, enlighten or deceive. Scripture declares, "Death and life are in the power of the tongue" (Proverbs 18:21), and nowhere is that truth more visible than in the systems of media that dominate our age.

The purpose of communication, in Heaven's design, is to convey truth. God is a communicator and His Word brought creation into being (Genesis 1:3). Every decree He issues sustains reality, and every word He speaks releases order, revelation, and light (Psalm 33:6; John 1:1–5). Humanity was given speech to reflect that divine nature - to speak truth in love (Ephesians 4:15), to declare the works of the Lord (Psalm 96:3), and to edify rather than corrupt (Ephesians 4:29). Media, therefore, was meant to be an extension of that creative communication - an instrument for spreading light, knowledge, and the testimony of truth throughout the earth.

Yet, as in every mountain, the adversary has corrupted what God intended for good. The Mountain of Media has become a strategic stronghold for deception. It no longer reflects light but manufactures illusion. Through false narratives, censorship, propaganda, and psychological manipulation, the enemy uses communication to enslave minds, divide nations, and distort truth. Lies are presented as facts, truth is branded as extremism, and public discourse has become a theater for spiritual warfare. The serpent who deceived Eve with words now whispers through airwaves and algorithms, seeking to rewrite reality itself (Genesis 3:1–5; John 8:44).

The Ekklesia, as the legislative voice of Heaven, carries the divine mandate to reclaim this mountain and reestablish the dominion of truth. The battle for media is not simply about information, but it is about governance of narrative. Whoever controls the narrative controls perception, and whoever controls perception, controls nations. The Ekklesia must therefore legislate truth into the communication structures of the earth, releasing the Spirit of Truth to displace the spirit of deception.

Ephesians 4:25 commands, "Therefore, putting away falsehood, let each one of you speak truth with his neighbor, for we are members one of another." Truth-telling is not optional. It is the moral foundation of the Kingdom. The psalmist adds, "He who walks uprightly, and works righteousness, and speaks the truth in his heart… he who does not slander with his tongue, nor does evil to his neighbor" (Psalm 15:2–3). When these principles govern communication, righteousness is exalted, and integrity becomes the standard of public discourse.

The Ekklesia must occupy the gates of this mountain - news, entertainment, journalism, film, digital media, and social networks - with prophetic authority. We are not called to echo the world's chaos, but to amplify Heaven's voice. Where falsehood has become systemic, we decree exposure. Where truth has been suppressed, we decree revelation. Every lie, every hidden agenda, and every manipulative narrative must be brought into the light of God's justice.

The Ekklesia also commissions righteous reformers within the media realm who carry the anointing of truth and excellence. These are the modern scribes of the Kingdom who will write, broadcast, and publish under the inspiration of the Spirit, restoring credibility and integrity to the flow of information. Their voices will become instruments of light in a culture of distortion.

As the Ekklesia legislates from Heaven's court, we decree that the airwaves and digital spaces will no longer serve as altars of confusion and corruption. We proclaim that every platform of communication must yield to the government of the Most High. Angels assigned to truth will war against spirits of deception, slander, and manipulation. Lies will collapse under the weight of divine exposure, and truth will rise as the plumb line of nations (Amos 7:7–8).

The Mountain of Media is not merely about technology or entertainment, but it is about the stewardship of truth. When truth governs communication, nations are illuminated. When deception rules, darkness spreads. The Ekklesia, as Heaven's voice in the earth, must ensure that the light of truth shines unhindered. For as it is written: "The light shines in the darkness, and the darkness has not overcome it" (John 1:5).

The restoration of this mountain will usher in a new era of prophetic communication—where media becomes a vessel of revelation, intercession, and transformation. The voice of the Lord will thunder through the airwaves once again, and the knowledge of His glory will cover the earth as the waters cover the sea (Habakkuk 2:14).

4. **The Mountain of Arts and Entertainment** mirrors the creative nature of God. It must glorify the Creator through beauty, purity, and prophetic expression rather than idolatry and perversion (Exodus 31:1–5; Philippians 4:8).

The restoration of this mountain will usher in a new era of prophetic communication—where media becomes a vessel of revelation, intercession, and transformation. The voice of the Lord will thunder through the airwaves once again, and the knowledge of His glory will cover the earth as the waters cover the sea (Habakkuk 2:14).

The Mountain of Arts and Entertainment is the sphere that shapes imagination, emotion, and culture through creativity and expression. It encompasses music, film, literature, design, theater, visual art, fashion, and performance. Each serves as a vehicle through which values are communicated and hearts are moved. This mountain has the unique power to capture the soul of a generation, to inspire nations, and to reveal unseen realities through image, sound, and story. It was created by God as a mirror of His own nature, for He is the Master Artist, the Author of beauty, and the Composer of creation itself (Genesis 1:1; Psalm 19:1; Exodus 31:1–5).

Art in its purest form is prophetic—it interprets divine truth through beauty and communicates spiritual reality through creative expression. When Bezalel and Oholiab were anointed by the Spirit of God to design the tabernacle, their craftsmanship was not mere artistry; it was worship (Exodus 31:1–5). Their creativity carried revelation. Every color, pattern, and sound testified of the glory of the unseen God. In the Kingdom, art is not entertainment for pleasure's sake—it is ministry that reveals the nature of the Creator.

However, when creativity is divorced from its divine source, it becomes a weapon of corruption. The enemy, who cannot create but only distort, has long sought to occupy this mountain to twist imagination into idolatry. He transforms beauty into vanity, passion into lust, and storytelling into deception. Through the arts, he has normalized rebellion, celebrated darkness, and desensitized humanity to sin. Entertainment has become an altar where fame is worshiped and the human ego enthroned. This is why the Ekklesia must rise to redeem creativity itself—to reclaim imagination as a holy instrument of revelation rather than manipulation.

The Mountain of Arts and Entertainment is one of the primary gates of influence in the earth. What is sung, shown, and shared becomes what societies believe. As songs shape memory, films mold identity, and imagery frames perception, the moral compass of entire generations is turned. The Ekklesia must therefore legislate over this mountain with discernment and authority, decreeing that the Spirit of Holiness governs creativity once again. For when this mountain is redeemed, it becomes one of the most powerful tools for evangelism, transformation, and the manifestation of glory in the earth.

Philippians 4:8 gives the Kingdom standard for artistic purity:

> "Whatever things are true, whatever things are honorable, whatever things are just, whatever things are pure, whatever things are lovely, whatever things are of good report—if there is any virtue and if there is anything praiseworthy—think on these things."

This is the plumb line of divine creativity. The arts must inspire hope, not despair; truth, not deception; beauty, not corruption. When the Spirit of God breathes upon human imagination, creativity becomes prophetic and it pierces darkness, awakens destiny, and glorifies the King.

The Ekklesia is Heaven's cultural architect, called to commission righteous creators who will build altars of beauty in a world marred by perversion. Musicians, writers, dancers, filmmakers, designers, and artists must be released under apostolic covering to reoccupy the stages, studios, and screens of culture. These are not entertainers, they are prophetic vessels, sent to reveal the beauty of holiness (Psalm 96:9) and the majesty of the King.

As Heaven's governing body, the Ekklesia must decree that this mountain be cleansed of the spirit of idolatry, rebellion, and seduction. The demonic principalities that have controlled music, media, and artistic influence must be dethroned. The sound of righteousness must rise to displace the noise of corruption. New genres, films, visual arts, and performances will emerge under the anointing of the Holy Spirit—filled with excellence, revelation, and transformative power. The anointing that rested on David's harp to drive out tormenting spirits (1 Samuel 16:23) will once again flow through Kingdom creatives who release healing, deliverance, and joy through their craft.

In this reformation, the Ekklesia becomes the curator of culture. It commissions art that testifies of the King's glory, funds creativity aligned with Heaven, and protects the integrity of prophetic expression from compromise. As the altars of Baal collapse in the entertainment world, the altar of worship will rise. Songs, films, and stories will once again carry the presence of God into the heart of nations. The world will witness beauty that does not seduce but sanctifies, creativity that does not distract but delivers, art that does not idolize man but enthrones Christ.

The Mountain of Arts and Entertainment was never meant to belong to darkness, but it belongs to the Creator and to those who bear His Spirit. The Ekklesia, as Heaven's governing council, now decrees that the Spirit of Truth, Beauty, and Holiness reigns over this sphere. Creativity will no longer glorify rebellion, but righteousness. No longer celebrate sin, but salvation. The earth will once again echo the symphony of the Creator's glory, and the nations will behold His beauty through the redeemed imagination of His sons and daughters.

5. **The Mountain of Economy** represents stewardship, provision, and resource distribution. It must be consecrated to the Lord, where wealth serves Kingdom purposes and justice governs commerce (Deuteronomy 8:18; Proverbs 13:22; Haggai 2:8).

The Mountain of Economy governs the flow of resources, trade, and wealth in the earth. It determines how nations prosper, how resources are distributed, and what systems sustain the lives of people and nations. Money itself is not evil - it is a tool, a neutral medium that reflects the values and priorities of those who steward it. Scripture reveals that "the silver is Mine, and the gold is Mine," says the Lord of hosts (Haggai 2:8). The economy, therefore, is not a manmade structure, but it is a divine trust. It was designed to function under Heaven's government, where wealth serves righteousness, and stewardship reflects the justice and generosity of the King.

From the beginning, God entrusted humanity with dominion that included resource management: "Be fruitful, multiply, fill the earth, and subdue it" (Genesis 1:28). Dominion was never ownership apart from God, but it was delegated authority within His covenant. The economy of the Kingdom is not built on greed or accumulation, but on stewardship and distribution - the just flow of provision from Heaven to humanity, from the righteous to the poor, from abundance to assignment. In this divine order, prosperity is not the goal, purpose is. Wealth exists to advance the will of God, empower His covenant people, and establish His covenant in the earth (Deuteronomy 8:18).

When this mountain is defiled, economies become instruments of oppression rather than justice. Systems driven by pride, greed, and exploitation replace stewardship with control. Debt becomes bondage, and manipulation of markets becomes modern sorcery. Mammon, the false god of material power, enthrones itself over nations, demanding allegiance through fear, lack, and competition (Matthew 6:24). Under Mammon's rule, wealth becomes a weapon that enslaves rather than liberates, concentrating power in the hands of a few while impoverishing the many. Yet Jesus declared that no one can serve both God and Mammon, for two masters cannot govern the same mountain. The Ekklesia must therefore confront and dethrone this principality through spiritual legislation, restoring divine order to the global economy.

The Ekklesia is the steward of Heaven's economy. It is not called merely to pray for provision but to legislate financial justice and release divine strategies of multiplication. The Ekklesia holds authority to call forth wealth from unrighteous systems and reassign it to Kingdom purposes, fulfilling the promise that "the wealth of the wicked is laid up for the just" (Proverbs 13:22). Through decrees and divine wisdom, the Ekklesia breaks the power of economic witchcraft, corruption, manipulation, inflation, and exploitation, and commands the realignment of commerce under the government of the Most High.

The biblical model for Kingdom economy is rooted in righteousness, generosity, and justice. In the early Church, no one lacked because resources were distributed according to need and purpose (Acts 4:32–35). Abraham's wealth was consecrated through covenant, Isaac's through obedience, Jacob's through revelation, and Joseph's through governance. Each patriarch demonstrated a dimension of divine economy - prosperity not for self, but for service. Joseph, especially, exemplifies the anointing of the Kingdom economist as one who interprets divine wisdom to preserve nations during famine (Genesis 41:39–57). That same anointing rests on the modern Ekklesia to design systems of resource distribution that break cycles of poverty, release innovation, and establish sustainable blessing in the earth.

Heaven's economy operates on the principles of faith, obedience, and integrity. When nations violate these principles through unjust weights and measures, predatory trade, or the exploitation of labor, they invoke judgment rather than blessing (Proverbs 11:1; Amos 8:4–7). The Ekklesia, standing as Heaven's court on earth, must legislate against such corruption, decreeing justice over markets, integrity over commerce, and divine favor over the righteous. We call for the restoration of ethical enterprise and the collapse of systems built on greed and manipulation.

The Spirit of the Lord is releasing new blueprints for Kingdom wealth transfer which include strategies of innovation, investment, and entrepreneurship birthed from the mind of Christ. These will empower the righteous to own and govern economic gates: banking, trade, technology, agriculture, and resource management. When the righteous rule, the people rejoice; when the wicked control the economy, the people groan (Proverbs 29:2). The Ekklesia's decree establishes the foundation for divine prosperity, not as luxury, but as leverage for Kingdom advancement.

In this hour, the Mountain of Economy must be consecrated to the Lord. Wealth must once again serve worship, not idolatry and generosity, not greed. The financial systems of the earth must yield to the justice of the King, who measures prosperity by stewardship, not accumulation. The Ekklesia, seated with Christ in authority, legislates that this mountain bow to the government of the Most High.

We decree that wealth shall flow according to righteousness, that resources shall be redistributed to fund revival, restore cities, and release innovation under divine mandate. We decree that Mammon's altars are dismantled, that financial corruption is exposed, and that divine provision is unlocked for the righteous. The days of economic captivity are over as the storehouses of Heaven are opening for those who steward according to covenant law.

The Mountain of Economy is being reclaimed by the Kingdom. Gold and silver will no longer serve rebellion but redemption and resources will no longer fund darkness but light. The Ekklesia will govern this mountain as Heaven's treasurers and faithful stewards of divine wealth, distributing provision for global harvest and generational blessing. For "the earth is the Lord's, and the fullness thereof" (Psalm 24:1), and all economies must now submit to His reign.

As these mountains are reclaimed, the dominion of Christ expands, and the nations are discipled according to the pattern of the Kingdom (Matthew 28:18–20; Isaiah 2:2–3).

Conclusion

Every decree within this collection is a legal proclamation issued from the Court of Heaven, framed in alignment with the Word and Spirit of God. These decrees are not ritualistic prayers but instruments of divine enforcement—binding what

Heaven forbids and loosing what Heaven sanctions (Matthew 16:19). When spoken by the righteous, they activate the angelic host (Psalm 103:20), dismantle demonic infrastructure (2 Corinthians 10:4–5), and establish the boundaries of righteousness within the earth.

These decrees are designed to equip the Ekklesia to function as a Kingdom government, legislating in the spiritual and natural realms. As they are released in faith, they activate Heaven's resources, enforce divine law, and realign territories with the original intent of God. Each decree is a strategic weapon of governance, enabling the Ekklesia to occupy its seat of authority until every mountain is brought under the lordship of Christ (Philippians 2:9–11; Daniel 7:27).

Let these decrees be released not as mere words, but as legal proclamations from Heaven's court. Let the Ekklesia arise in her full governmental authority—united, discerning, and courageous—to legislate righteousness, overthrow demonic systems, and establish the Kingdom of God in every sphere of influence.

For the Ekklesia is not a passive church—it is the ruling government of Heaven on earth. Through her decrees, Heaven's justice is released, nations are reformed, and the glory of the Lord fills the earth as the waters cover the sea (Habakkuk 2:14).

These decrees are weapons placed in the hands of the Ekklesia, yet they are not a substitute for your own watchful listening before the Lord. Every believer must continue to seek Heaven's voice, receive fresh instruction, and draw down the strategies and blueprints assigned to them for this moment in history.

At the same time, let this collection serve as a battle-ready war manual—a resource to equip the saints for governmental engagement and high-level spiritual warfare. These decrees model the language, structure, and legal foundations of effective Kingdom legislation so that intercessors, watchmen, and leaders are trained to craft their own Spirit-led decrees.

May these pages sharpen your understanding, strengthen your authority, and empower you to develop personalized decrees as the Holy Spirit unveils strategies specific to your assignment, sphere, and territory.

ARTS & ENTERTAINMENT

1. **Sanctification of Creativity and Imagination**

    - Recognition of God as the original Creator and Source of artistic inspiration.
    - Restoration of purity, truth, and divine purpose in creative expression.

2. **Cleansing of Cultural Gates and Platforms**

    - Purification of the arts, film, music, and entertainment industries from perversion, idolatry, and occult influence.
    - Reclaiming cultural influence for righteousness and truth.

3. **Freedom of Expression under Righteous Standards**

    - Defending artistic freedom guided by conscience and moral law.
    - Prohibiting coercion or censorship of godly expression in the arts.

4. **Righteous Representation and Storytelling**

    - Replacing narratives of darkness, rebellion, and despair with those of redemption, honor, and hope.
    - Empowering creators to reflect the image and glory of God through their craft.

5. **Economic and Structural Reformation of the Industry**

    - Dismantling corrupt entertainment systems built on exploitation and greed.

- Establishing righteous infrastructure for Kingdom-based production and distribution.

6. **Generational Protection and Cultural Renewal**
    - Guarding children and youth from immoral and destructive entertainment.
    - Releasing revival in music, film, fashion, and the arts that awakens nations to righteousness.

7. **Global Witness of Glory through the Arts**
    - Commissioning artists, musicians, and storytellers as prophetic voices to the nations.
    - Declaring the global return of creativity to the service of the Creator.

AUTHORITIES FOR THE ARTS & ENTERTAINMENT MOUNTAIN DECREES

CONSTITUTIONAL AUTHORITY

- **First Amendment, U.S. Constitution (1791):** "Congress shall make no law… abridging the freedom of speech."

- **Declaration of Independence (1776):** "All men are created equal, that they are endowed by their Creator with certain unalienable Rights…"

- **Article I, Section 8:** Empowering citizens to secure rights over creative works ("To promote the Progress of Science and useful Arts…").

Biblical Authority

- *Genesis 1:1 – "In the beginning God created the heavens and the earth."*

- *Exodus 35:31–32 – "He has filled him with the Spirit of God, in wisdom, in understanding, in knowledge, and in all manner of workmanship."*

- *Psalm 33:3 – "Sing to Him a new song; play skillfully with a shout of joy."*

- *Exodus 31:2–4 – "See, I have called by name Bezalel… to design artistic works."*

- *Isaiah 60:1 – "Arise, shine; for your light has come, and the glory of the Lord is risen upon you."*

- *Philippians 4:8 – "Whatever things are true, whatever things are noble… think on these things."*

- *Psalm 96:3 – "Declare His glory among the nations, His wonders among all peoples."*

- *Revelation 21:26 – "They shall bring the glory and the honor of the nations into it."*

PRAYER

Righteous Judge, Master Creator, and Author of Beauty, we come before Your throne concerning the Mountain of Arts and Entertainment. You are the Source of all creativity, and You designed art to reveal Your glory, communicate truth, and awaken the hearts of nations. We acknowledge that this mountain has been polluted by pride, lust, greed, and idolatry, but You are redeeming it for Your Kingdom.

We present Your Word as evidence that You fill craftsmen, writers, musicians, and visionaries with divine skill and inspiration. We appeal for verdicts against the spirits of perversion, deception, and corruption that have defiled the cultural gates. Let the altars of human worship and celebrity be torn down, and let Your presence reclaim the stages, studios, and screens of the world.

Raise up artists filled with Your Spirit—prophetic voices who paint, sing, write, and produce by revelation and truth. Let the arts once again declare the glory of the Lord and disciple nations through beauty, excellence, and holiness.

We decree the reclamation of this mountain for the Kingdom of God. Let light invade darkness, and let every creative work glorify Jesus Christ, the true Creator. So be it.

DECREES

We decree that the Spirit of the Creator is released upon artists, musicians, writers, and storytellers to manifest divine beauty and truth.

We prohibit the use of art, music, film, and culture to glorify evil, promote perversion, or exalt darkness.

We decree that creative expression is sanctified, reflecting the image and nature of the Most High God.

We call forth a new wave of anointed creators who release sounds, stories, and designs from the throne of Heaven.

We decree that every altar of idolatry, celebrity worship, and occultism in the entertainment industry is dismantled.

We prohibit the exploitation of people and creation for profit, lust, or manipulation.

We decree that music, film, and media are cleansed from demonic influence and restored to righteousness.

We release the fire of God into the entertainment capitals of the world to purify and reclaim them for His glory.

We decree that every hidden network of trafficking, abuse, and corruption within the industry is exposed and destroyed.

We prohibit the sexualization and exploitation of children through entertainment, fashion, or advertising.

We decree that purity, virtue, and family values return to film, music, and storytelling.

We deploy Angel Armies to guard creative gates and silence demonic voices seeking to shape culture through lies.

We decree that Kingdom artists receive divine favor, funding, and open doors to influence global platforms.

We prohibit censorship of righteous art or persecution of creators who honor God's truth.

We decree that new creative hubs and studios arise, dedicated to producing works of redemption, excellence, and light.

We decree that worship and prophetic art shall flood cities, transforming atmospheres and healing hearts.

We decree that the arts become an instrument of evangelism and awakening in this generation.

We prohibit the glorification of death, violence, and immorality in cultural production.

We decree that storylines of hope, honor, and justice replace narratives of rebellion, despair, and corruption.

We summon skilled craftsmen and artisans like Bezalel and Oholiab, filled with the Spirit of Wisdom for Kingdom creativity.

We decree that composers, designers, and performers encounter the living God and use their gifts for His glory.

We prohibit the counterfeit spirit of fame and pride from possessing the hearts of artists and leaders in the creative world.

We decree that the arts become a prophetic instrument of healing, unity, and revival among the nations.

We call forth a global movement of creativity led by the Spirit of God that will release beauty, truth, and transformation.

We decree that the Mountain of Arts & Entertainment is redeemed by the blood of Jesus, filled with His glory, and restored to its original mandate—to reveal the splendor of the Creator and declare His praise among the nations.

We decree that the breath of the Almighty fills studios, stages, galleries, and screens, transforming them into sanctuaries where the presence of God abides.

We decree that divine imagination is unlocked within creators, releasing new genres, designs, and sounds that carry revelation from the throne.

We decree that truth and beauty intertwine as instruments of divine persuasion, turning hearts toward righteousness and wonder.

We decree that every artistic gatekeeper now comes under Heaven's authority, stewarding influence in humility and purity.

We decree that artistic innovation flows through the Spirit of Wisdom, producing excellence that eclipses counterfeit glory.

We decree that sacred creativity invades secular arenas, dismantling the myth of separation between holy and cultural spaces.

We decree that the eyes and ears of audiences are anointed to discern light from darkness and to hunger for truth over entertainment.

We decree that lyrics, scripts, and imagery are inspired by revelation knowledge rather than rebellion or despair.

We decree that fashion, architecture, and design reveal the order and majesty of the Creator instead of vanity and excess.

We decree that the voices of righteous influencers rise with boldness to confront corruption and proclaim virtue in public forums.

We decree that prophetic creativity awakens nations to destiny, releasing healing to traumatized cultures and divided peoples.

We decree that artistic communities are filled with the fear of the Lord, cultivating honor, and moral clarity.

We decree that digital and technological creativity serve the Gospel, advancing communication, worship, and education for Kingdom purpose.

We decree that the generational mantle of artistry is passed to sons and daughters who will carry purity, innovation, and glory beyond this era.

We decree that the sound of Heaven resounds through America's creative gates, proclaiming, *"The earth is the Lord's and the fullness thereof,"* until every medium and melody reveals His splendor.

IT IS SO ORDERED.

BUSINESS AND ECONOMY MOUNTAIN

1. **Divine Ownership and Stewardship**

   - Recognition that the earth and all wealth belong to the Lord.
   - Restoration of righteous stewardship and accountability in commerce.

2. **Integrity, Justice, and Righteous Trade**

   - Establishing honesty, fairness, and transparency in all economic dealings.
   - Breaking systems of exploitation, greed, and corruption.

3. **Freedom and Prosperity under Kingdom Principles**

   - Affirming free enterprise and wealth creation aligned with biblical wisdom.
   - Protecting against socialism, economic tyranny, and manipulation.

4. **Wealth Transfer and Kingdom Finance**

   - Decreeing that resources flow from wicked systems to the hands of the righteous.
   - Commissioning entrepreneurs and innovators for Kingdom expansion.

5. **Labor, Dignity, and Provision**

   - Honoring the worker and restoring balance between profit, people, and purpose.

- Breaking cycles of poverty, oppression, and exploitation of labor.

6. **Economic Justice and Freedom from Debt**

- Dismantling unjust systems of usury, inflation, and debt bondage.
- Releasing divine strategies for financial deliverance and stewardship.

7. **Global Economic Reformation**

- Establishing righteous trade among nations and dismantling corrupt financial empires.
- Declaring Christ as Lord over all economies, currencies, and markets.

AUTHORITIES FOR THE BUSINESS & ECONOMY MOUNTAIN DECREES

CONSTITUTIONAL AUTHORITY

Article I, Section 8, U.S. Constitution: Congress shall have power "to regulate commerce… and to coin money."

Fifth Amendment: "No person shall be deprived of life, liberty, or property, without due process of law."

Declaration of Independence: The right to "life, liberty, and the pursuit of happiness," which includes enterprise and ownership under divine blessing.

Biblical Authority

- *Psalm 24:1 – "The earth is the Lord's, and all its fullness, the world and those who dwell therein."*

- *Deuteronomy 8:18 – "It is He who gives you power to get wealth, that He may establish His covenant."*

- *Proverbs 11:1 – "Dishonest scales are an abomination to the Lord, but a just weight is His delight."*

- *Leviticus 19:35–36 – "You shall do no injustice in judgment, in measurement of length, weight, or volume."*

- *Proverbs 13:22 – "The wealth of the sinner is stored up for the righteous."*

- *Isaiah 60:5 – "The wealth of the nations shall come to you."*

- *2 Thessalonians 3:10 – "If anyone will not work, neither shall he eat."*

- *Colossians 3:23–24 – "Whatever you do, do it heartily, as to the Lord and not to men."*

- *Nehemiah 5:11 – "Restore now to them… their fields, their vineyards, their olive groves, and their houses."*

- *Philippians 4:19 – "My God shall supply all your need according to His riches in glory by Christ Jesus."*

PRAYER

Righteous Judge, Owner of all creation, and King over the nations, we come before Your throne to present the Mountain of Business and Economy. You established work, trade, and stewardship as expressions of dominion, not oppression. You have declared that the power to get wealth comes from You, that Your covenant may be established in the earth.

We present as evidence Your Word and the founding principles of this nation, which affirm liberty, private property, and the right to prosper under righteous labor. We ask for judgments against greed, corruption, exploitation, and manipulation that defile economies and enslave generations. Let every ungodly system built on oppression, theft, or deception be judged and dismantled.

We appeal for verdicts that release Kingdom entrepreneurs, innovators, and reformers filled with integrity and wisdom. Let righteous trade, innovation, and creativity flow freely, releasing prosperity for the advancement of the Gospel. May economies align with Heaven's government and reflect Your justice, generosity, and abundance. So be it.

DECREES

We decree that the earth and all its resources belong to the Lord, and that He appoints righteous stewards over His wealth.

We prohibit the manipulation of markets, currencies, and resources for evil or unjust gain.

We decree that honesty, integrity, and truth govern all trade, contracts, and financial dealings.

We release a cleansing fire through corporate, financial, and governmental systems to expose corruption and greed.

We decree that righteous business leaders arise who steward wealth for Kingdom advancement and societal good.

We prohibit exploitation of laborers, deceitful accounting, and unjust profit gained through manipulation or coercion.

We decree that entrepreneurship flourishes under divine wisdom, creativity, and innovation.

We summon divine strategies for sustainable wealth creation rooted in righteousness and generosity.

We decree that the wealth of the wicked is transferred into the hands of the righteous to establish covenant purposes.

We prohibit demonic dynasties, monopolies, cartels, and unlawful alliances that enslave markets or control resources for evil.

We decree that freedom of enterprise and property ownership are protected under Heaven's constitution and national law.

We decree the restoration of lands, inheritances, and generational wealth lost through deception or corruption.

We decree that economies are cleansed from debt slavery and inflationary systems that oppress the poor.

We prohibit predatory lending, usury, and financial enslavement that violates divine justice.

We decree that just weights and measures return to financial systems and trade among nations.

We decree that Kingdom financiers, investors, and economists anointed with Joseph's wisdom shall rebuild in righteousness.

We decree that Kingdom businesses honor God, value people, and advance purpose above profit.

We prohibit unethical practices, trafficking, and exploitation in all supply chains and industries.

We decree that divine favor and creativity rest on Kingdom entrepreneurs to birth new industries of light.

We deploy Angel Armies to war against the principalities of Mammon and greed in global markets.

We decree that corruption in banking, trade, and taxation is exposed, judged, and replaced with righteous systems.

We prohibit economic sabotage, theft of intellectual property, and manipulation through digital or AI systems.

We decree that giving, generosity, and covenant partnership release supernatural provision for Kingdom purposes.

We decree a global reformation of economics that honors God's design for stewardship, abundance, and justice.

We decree that the Mountain of Business & Economy is redeemed under the Lordship of Jesus Christ, governed by righteousness, and filled with the glory of His prosperity until the nations are discipled through divine commerce.

We decree that the breath of the Almighty overshadows every creative contract, compelling integrity, equity, and righteous stewardship of resources.

We decree that every soundtrack, script, and production conceived in secret darkness is brought into light and judged by truth.

We decree that creative technologies—virtual, digital, and visual—submit to the Lordship of Christ and serve the advancement of light.

We decree that the anointing of craftsmanship returns to cities once known for depravity, converting them into centers of holy innovation.

We decree that divine timing governs all artistic release so that Heaven's message is never delayed or prematurely silenced.

We decree that creative awards, honors, and platforms become testimonies of grace rather than monuments of pride.

We decree that the atmosphere of rehearsals, recording rooms, and studios is sanctified by the presence of the Holy Spirit.

We decree that every exploitative contract or oath signed in deceit is rendered null by the blood of the Lamb.

We decree that storytellers receive dreams and visions from the Ancient of Days that reveal His redemptive plan for nations.

We decree that artistic unions and guilds operate in justice, valuing workers as image-bearers rather than commodities.

We decree that philanthropic wealth within the arts is redirected to fund righteous creativity and humanitarian restoration.

We decree that sound engineers, editors, and producers discern truth in frequencies and images, filtering out corruption.

We decree that museums, galleries, and cultural centers become altars of remembrance where God's beauty confronts despair.

We decree that angelic guardians stand watch over creative portals—film festivals, streaming networks, and global showcases—to restrain evil and release light.

We decree that prophetic art heals trauma, breaking mental torment and releasing peace to those who encounter it.

We decree that artistic competition yields to collaboration under Kingdom order, producing unity without compromise.

We decree that nations exchange righteous creativity—songs, literature, and design—that testify of the glory of God across borders.

We decree that counterfeit inspiration drawn from sorcery, hallucinogens, or divination collapses under the weight of holiness.

We decree that the hearts of producers, investors, and decision-makers are turned toward righteousness, favoring projects that exalt truth.

We decree that every artistic sphere in America bows to the supremacy of Christ, the True Light, whose glory now governs imagination, commerce, and culture. IT IS SO ORDERED.

EDUCATION MOUNTAIN

1. **Truth & Wisdom as the Foundation of Learning**

   - Restoration of truth, integrity, and reverence for God as the source of all wisdom.
   - Rejection of deception, revisionism, and ideological indoctrination.

2. **Parents as Primary Educators**

   - Affirmation of parental authority in the moral, spiritual, and intellectual formation of their children.
   - Protection of families from state or institutional overreach into child education.

3. **Freedom of Thought, Conscience, and Faith in Academia**

   - Safeguarding freedom of speech, religious expression, and open inquiry in schools and universities.
   - Protection against censorship and discrimination based on biblical worldview.

4. **Purity and Protection of the Next Generation**

   - Shielding students from sexualization, grooming, or manipulation of identity.
   - Ensuring education honors innocence, virtue, and moral formation.

5. **Curriculum of Truth and National Honor**

- Restoration of accurate history, biblical literacy, and moral foundation in education.
- Prohibition of anti-God, anti-family, and anti-nation narratives.

6. **Anointing and Integrity in Educators**

- Raising up teachers filled with the Spirit of wisdom and truth.
- Purifying the educational system from corruption, compromise, and ideological control.

7. **Kingdom Education and Global Discipleship**

- Establishing Kingdom-based schools, universities, and educational movements worldwide.
- Decreeing that the knowledge of the Lord fills the earth through teaching, training, and truth.

AUTHORITIES FOR THE EDUCATION MOUNTAIN DECREES

CONSTITUTIONAL AUTHORITY

- **First Amendment, U.S. Constitution (1791):** "Congress shall make no law… abridging the freedom of speech."

- **14th Amendment, Section 1:** "No State shall deprive any person of life, liberty, or property, without due process of law."

- **Supreme Court –** *Pierce v. Society of Sisters* **(1925):** "The child is not the mere creature of the State; those who nurture him and direct his destiny have the right and high duty to prepare him for additional obligations."

BIBLICAL AUTHORITY

- *Proverbs 9:10 – "The fear of the Lord is the beginning of wisdom."*

- *John 8:32 – "And you shall know the truth, and the truth shall make you free."*

- *Deuteronomy 6:6–7 – "You shall teach them diligently to your children."*

- *Proverbs 22:6 – "Train up a child in the way he should go, and when he is old he will not depart from it."*

- *Philippians 4:8 – "Whatever things are true, whatever things are noble… meditate on these things."*

- *2 Timothy 3:16 – "All Scripture is given by inspiration of God, and is profitable for doctrine, for reproof, for correction, for instruction in righteousness."*

- *Isaiah 54:13 – "All your children shall be taught by the Lord, and great shall be the peace of your children."*

- *Matthew 28:19–20 – "Go therefore and make disciples of all nations… teaching them to observe all things that I have commanded you."*

PRAYER

Righteous Judge, Eternal Teacher, and Source of all truth, we come before Your throne to present the Mountain of Education. You alone are the Author of wisdom, and from Your mouth come knowledge and understanding. We acknowledge that education apart from You produces pride, confusion, and deception, but education rooted in You brings life, liberty, and truth.

We present as evidence the covenantal right of parents to train their children, the constitutional right to free thought and speech, and the biblical mandate to instruct in righteousness. We appeal for judgments against ideologies, systems, and spirits that pervert knowledge, corrupt innocence, and exalt lies against truth.

We ask You to raise up educators filled with wisdom, courage, and prophetic insight who will teach truth without compromise. Establish righteous curricula, restore virtue in the classroom, and cleanse every institution from deception and darkness.

We decree that the education systems of this land and the nations come under the Lordship of Christ, the true Teacher. Let truth prevail, wisdom be exalted, and every false ideology collapse under the weight of divine light.

In Jesus Christ's name — the Wisdom of God. So be it.

DECREES

We decree that the fear of the Lord is restored as the foundation of all knowledge and instruction in this nation.

We prohibit the exaltation of humanism, atheism, and godless ideologies within educational systems.

We decree that truth, integrity, and virtue replace deception, confusion, and moral relativism in every classroom.

We decree that the Spirit of Wisdom and Revelation shall rest upon teachers, students, and administrators.

We decree that parents are the primary authority over the education of their children, as ordained by God.

We prohibit governmental, corporate, or ideological interference that seeks to indoctrinate children or replace parental guidance.

We decree that every hidden curriculum promoting perversion, rebellion, or anti-God agendas is exposed and dismantled.

We deploy Angel Armies to surround schools, protecting children from evil influence, manipulation, and harm.

We decree that teachers and administrators walk in righteousness, teaching truth and modeling integrity.

We prohibit the use of education as a weapon to manipulate thought, silence faith, or enforce allegiance to false doctrines.

We decree that students shall encounter the Spirit of Truth and discern error, deceit, and manipulation.

We call forth reformers and revivalists into education to rebuild foundations of wisdom, truth, and moral excellence.

We decree that history is taught truthfully, honoring God's providence and the covenantal foundations of nations.

We prohibit the rewriting or erasure of historical truth for ideological or political agendas.

We decree that the innocence of children is protected from sexualization, gender confusion, and immoral propaganda.

We decree that divine order and purity shall cleanse schools and universities from demonic doctrines.

We decree that every lie exalting itself against the knowledge of God in academia is torn down.

We prohibit censorship of biblical worldview, truth-based science, or moral conviction in education.

We decree that campuses become centers of light, truth, and discovery under the wisdom of the Holy Spirit.

We summon kingdom educators and reformers to establish righteous schools, colleges, and training centers across the earth.

We decree that funding and favor are released to godly educational institutions aligned with Kingdom truth.

We prohibit demonic infiltration through false accreditation, curriculum control, or financial coercion.

We decree that a new generation of Daniels, Josephs, and Esthers arise from classrooms filled with revelation and courage.

We call forth global discipleship movements to teach nations the ways of the Lord and restore truth to every culture.

We decree that the mountain of Education is redeemed, aligned with Christ, and filled with the glory of divine wisdom, that the knowledge of the Lord covers the earth as the waters cover the sea.

We decree that the spirit of discernment saturates every mind, empowering learners to distinguish eternal truth from temporary opinion.

We decree that divine creativity invades instruction, unveiling solutions from Heaven for science, medicine, technology, and governance.

We decree that schools and universities become greenhouses of destiny where gifts, callings, and innovation mature under the fear of the Lord.

We decree that spiritual awakening sweeps through teachers' lounges, lecture halls, and research institutions until reverence replaces arrogance.

We decree that the anointing of understanding disarms confusion, bringing clarity and peace to students burdened by anxiety and deception.

We decree that righteous mentorship networks rise up to train youth in wisdom, virtue, and leadership for every sphere of culture.

We decree that divine order governs educational boards and policies, expelling corruption, compromise, and godless influence.

We decree that revelation knowledge transforms outdated systems, releasing modern parables that reveal eternal principles through learning.

We decree that the language of instruction is purified, free from profanity, deceit, and blasphemy, seasoned instead with grace and truth.

We decree that supernatural wisdom equips inventors and thinkers to pioneer breakthroughs that serve humanity and glorify God.

We decree that the covenant between family and faith-based education is strengthened, creating an unbroken cord of truth across generations.

We decree that angelic scribes record and preserve the testimonies of transformed classrooms as witness to future nations.

We decree that divine justice is rendered against corruption in testing, admissions, and scholarship systems, restoring equity and honor.

We decree that a spirit of excellence distinguishes godly educators, setting them as examples and advisors to leaders of nations.

We decree that the revelation of Christ as Logos—the Living Word—fills the halls of learning, and that wisdom from above becomes the governing standard of all education.

IT IS SO ORDERED.

FAMILY MOUNTAIN

1. **Sanctity of Marriage and Covenant**

    • Defending biblical marriage as a covenant between one man and one woman.
    • Restoring fidelity and covenant love in homes.

2. **Parental Authority and Legacy**

    • Protecting parents' divine right to guide their children.
    • Guarding against state intrusion into the family unit.

3. **Protection of Children and Generational Continuity**

    • Safeguarding children from harm, indoctrination, and identity confusion.
    • Establishing blessing, identity, and inheritance in Christ.

4. **Restoration of Family Order**

    • Aligning households under God's design of love and leadership.
    • Healing division, fatherlessness, and generational pain.

5. **Freedom from Destruction Agendas**

    • Breaking spirits of divorce, abortion, and family disintegration.
    • Defending the family as the cornerstone of national strength.

6. **Economic and Territorial Blessing**

   • Releasing divine provision and stewardship over family inheritance.
   • Breaking poverty cycles and debt bondage.

7. **National Witness of Righteous Families**

   • Raising families as living testimonies of God's covenant and Kingdom order.

AUTHORITIES FOR THE FAMILY MOUNTAIN DECREES

CONSTITUTIONAL AUTHORITY:

• **Ninth Amendment, U.S. Constitution (1791)**

"The enumeration in the Constitution, of certain rights, shall not be construed to deny or disparage others retained by the people."

• **Fourteenth Amendment, Section 1, U.S. Constitution (1868)**

"All persons born or naturalized in the United States, and subject to the jurisdiction thereof, are citizens of the United States and of the State wherein they reside.

No State shall make or enforce any law which shall abridge the privileges or immunities of citizens of the United States;

nor shall any State deprive any person of life, liberty, or property, without due process of law;

nor deny to any person within its jurisdiction the equal protection of the laws."

- **Supreme Court of the United States — Pierce v. Society of Sisters, 268 U.S. 510 (1925)**

"The child is not the mere creature of the State; those who nurture him and direct his destiny have the right, coupled with the high duty, to recognize and prepare him for additional obligations."

BIBLICAL AUTHORITY:

- *Genesis 2:24 - "Therefore a man shall leave his father and mother and be joined to his wife, and they shall become one flesh."*

- *Matthew 19:6 – "So then, they are no longer two but one flesh. Therefore what God has joined together, let not man separate."*

- *Deuteronomy 6:6–7 – "And these words which I command you today shall be in your heart. You shall teach them diligently to your children, and shall talk of them when you sit in your house, when you walk by the way, when you lie down, and when you rise up."*

- *Ephesians 6:4 – "And you, fathers, do not provoke your children to wrath, but bring them up in the training and admonition of the Lord."*

- *Psalm 127:3 – "Behold, children are a heritage from the Lord, the fruit of the womb is a reward."*

- *Malachi 4:6 – "And he will turn the hearts of the fathers to the children, and the hearts of the children to their fathers, lest I come and strike the earth with a curse."*

- *Joshua 24:15 – "And if it seems evil to you to serve the Lord, choose for yourselves this day whom you will serve… But as for me and my house, we will serve the Lord."*

- *Proverbs 22:6 – "Train up a child in the way he should go, and when he is old he will not depart from it."*

- *Proverbs 13:22 – "A good man leaves an inheritance to his children's children, but the wealth of the sinner is stored up for the righteous."*

- *Exodus 20:12 – "Honor your father and your mother, that your days may be long upon the land which the Lord your God is giving you."*

PRAYER

Heavenly Father and Righteous Judge, we present the family—Your first institution—before Your throne. You established the home before nations, and You ordained marriage as a covenant reflection of Christ and His Bride. We petition for judgment against every power that seeks to destroy covenant love, corrupt children, or pervert identity.

Let homes be sanctuaries of Your presence and centers of revival. Heal generations, restore fathers to sons and mothers to daughters, and rebuild the altars of family worship across this land. So be it.

DECREES

We decree from the Throne of Eternal Covenant that marriage between one man and one woman is a holy reflection of Christ and His Bride, established before time, protected by divine law, and sealed in blood.

We prohibit every counterfeit definition of union, for the Verdict of Creation has already been rendered: "Male and female He created them." We enforce that verdict across time, culture, and governance.

We decree that covenant fidelity and marital unity are not being restored—they stand unbroken in Heaven's record. We call earth to mirror that eternal oneness.

We decree that the river of reconciliation from the Throne of Mercy shall flow through broken homes, healing breaches and binding hearts into divine order.

We decree that parents carry divine stewardship over their children as extensions of God's image, not subjects of the State. The authority of motherhood and fatherhood is ordained and guarded by Heaven's government.

We prohibit any decree of man that seeks to sever or substitute parental governance, for Heaven's constitution declares, "The child is not the creature of the State."

We decree that fathers rise as image-bearers of the Heavenly Father—governing in love, protection, and strength—and that mothers move in grace and nurture under the mantle of wisdom.

We release the fire from the altar before the Throne to reignite family altars of worship in homes across America, where covenant presence is restored and generations commune before the Lord.

We decree that children are sanctified in truth, shielded by the blood of the Lamb, and governed by angelic protection from every form of indoctrination, abuse, and exploitation.

We prohibit trafficking, grooming, and manipulation of children, enforcing Heaven's ruling that "Whoever harms one of these little ones" is already condemned under divine justice.

We decree that family identity is found only in Christ, the eternal Son, and that every counterfeit identity is dissolved in the revelation of sonship.

We decree the Spirit of Adoption from the heart of the Father shall flood this generation—restoring belonging, healing rejection, and binding hearts to divine lineage.

We decree that the spirit of divorce and covenant-breaking is judged at the Cross. We enforce that verdict now: covenant love triumphs over division.

We prohibit the operation of Molech—the destroyer of children—and decree the end of abortion, infanticide, and every ideology of death; for the blood of Jesus speaks a better word over this land.

We decree that households prosper because Heaven's economy is governed by generosity, covenant, and obedience—not by mammon or fear.

We decree generational blessing already written in the Lamb's Book of Life shall flow unhindered—legacy restored, inheritance recovered, and lineage realigned.

We decree that debt, oppression, and economic bondage bow to the Jubilee verdict of Christ's finished work. Freedom is the law of His Kingdom.

We prohibit demonic cycles of poverty, addiction, and violence, for the Prince of Peace rules every home submitted to His Lordship.

We decree that families disciple nations, releasing righteousness, wisdom, and love as the governing pattern of the Kingdom on earth.

We decree that revival fire from the throne of the Most High shall dwell in homes transforming kitchens into sanctuaries, tables into altars, and families into assemblies of glory.

We decree that every home becomes a dwelling place of the manifest presence of God, for the tabernacle of God is with men.

We prohibit rebellion, dishonor, and destruction, enforcing Heaven's verdict that peace and order reign under Christ's headship.

We decree that the orphan spirit is displaced by the Spirit of Sonship; no child, parent, or generation remains estranged from divine family.

We decree that the oil of joy replaces mourning, and unity replaces division, as Heaven's harmony fills every household in this land.

We decree, from the seat of government in Christ, that the Mountain of Family in the United States stands restored under the Lamb's authority, sealed in covenant, radiant in glory, and operating in the eternal design of the Father, Son, and Holy Spirit.

We decree that the blueprint of family established in the councils of eternity is now made manifest in the earth, unmarred by the distortions of time or culture.

We decree that love rooted in divine truth expels fear, heals memory, and forms the atmosphere of every household.

We decree that every marriage functions as a prophetic picture of Christ's unbreakable covenant with His Bride, releasing glory into communities and generations.

We decree that divine order in the home releases governmental stability in the nation, for the microcosm of family mirrors the macrocosm of Kingdom rule.

We decree that grace and truth intertwine at family tables, reconciling generations through shared wisdom and humility.

We decree that the song of redemption resounds in family lineages, silencing generational shame and trauma.

We decree that mothers carry the mantle of nurture that births destiny, while fathers release covering and vision that sustain legacy.

We decree that sons and daughters arise in purity and purpose, clothed in the honor of obedience and the joy of belonging.

We decree that laughter, celebration, and thanksgiving return as marks of holy habitation within American homes.

We decree that every inheritance—spiritual, intellectual, material—is stewarded in righteousness and multiplied for Kingdom advancement.

We decree that wisdom from above governs family decisions, replacing confusion with clarity and contention with peace.

We decree that households become embassies of Heaven where hospitality, generosity, and intercession converge.

We decree that prophetic vision for families is renewed, guiding them to build, plant, and occupy according to divine timing.

We decree that angelic guardians assigned to family covenants are loosed to secure boundaries, protect destinies, and enforce blessing.

We decree that the fragrance of holiness fills homes, consecrating domestic spaces as sanctuaries of presence and praise.

IT IS SO ORDERED.

GOVERNMENT MOUNTAIN

1. **Divine Order & Sovereignty**

   - Acknowledging God as the supreme Lawgiver, Judge, and King.
   - Aligning human government under divine law and moral order.

2. **Righteous Leadership & Integrity in Office**

   - Establishing truth, justice, and righteousness as the foundation of governance.
   - Exposing and removing corruption, bribery, and deceit.

3. **Constitutional Protection & Rule of Law**

   - Preserving constitutional government and separation of powers.
   - Restraining tyranny, overreach, and lawlessness in every branch.

4. **Justice & Righteous Legislation**

   - Ensuring laws align with God's moral standards.
   - Dismantling unrighteous decrees and unjust judgments.

5. **Civic Freedom & Protection of the People**

   - Upholding the God-given rights of citizens: life, liberty, and property.
   - Protecting against exploitation, censorship, and unlawful control.

6. **Purity in Election & Representation**

- Defending honest elections and truth in leadership selection.
- Overturning fraud, manipulation, and deceit in governance.

7. **Global Governmental Alignment with the Kingdom**

- Calling nations into righteous alignment with Christ's eternal dominion.
- Declaring His Kingdom government above every throne and power.

AUTHORITIES FOR THE GOVERNMENT MOUNTAIN DECREES

CONSTITUTIONAL AUTHORITY

- Preamble, U.S. Constitution: "To establish justice, insure domestic tranquility, provide for the common defense, promote the general welfare, and secure the blessings of liberty to ourselves and our posterity."

- Article VI, Clause 2 – Supremacy Clause: "This Constitution… shall be the supreme law of the land."

- Declaration of Independence (1776): "That all men are created equal, that they are endowed by their Creator with certain unalienable Rights… That to secure these rights, Governments are instituted among Men."

BIBLICAL AUTHORITY

- *Isaiah 33:22 – "For the Lord is our Judge, the Lord is our Lawgiver, the Lord is our King; He will save us."*

- *Psalm 22:28 – "For the kingdom is the Lord's, and He rules over the nations."*

- *Proverbs 29:2 – "When the righteous are in authority, the people rejoice; but when a wicked man rules, the people groan."*

- *2 Samuel 23:3 – "He who rules over men must be just, ruling in the fear of God."*

- *Isaiah 1:26 – "I will restore your judges as at the first, and your counselors as at the beginning."*

- *Amos 5:24 – "But let justice run down like water, and righteousness like a mighty stream."*

- *Proverbs 12:22 – "Lying lips are an abomination to the Lord, but those who deal truthfully are His delight."*

- *Exodus 18:21 – "Select capable men from all the people—men who fear God, trustworthy men who hate dishonest gain."*

- *Daniel 2:21 – "He removes kings and raises up kings."*

- *Revelation 11:15 – "The kingdoms of this world have become the kingdoms of our Lord and of His Christ."*

PRAYER

Righteous Judge and Sovereign King, we come before Your throne presenting the Mountain of Government. You are the origin of all authority, and every ruler stands accountable before Your court. You establish kings and remove them, and You alone hold the scepter of true government.

We present the founding documents of this nation as witness: that government was ordained to secure rights granted by You, not to usurp them. We acknowledge that just governance flows from righteousness, truth, and accountability to divine law.

We petition Your court to render judgment against corruption, tyranny, and lawlessness. Expose every hidden alliance, dark counsel, and unjust decree that perverts justice.

Establish righteous rulers, restore constitutional order, and align this government with Heaven's government.

Let every law and policy reflect Your truth, and let every leader govern with the fear of the Lord. We appeal for divine intervention and angelic enforcement to cleanse, reform, and reestablish this nation's foundations in righteousness.

In the name of Jesus Christ, King of kings and Lord of lords. So be it.

DECREES

We decree that the government of this nation rests upon the shoulders of Christ, the Wonderful Counselor, Mighty God, Everlasting Father, and Prince of Peace.

We prohibit the exaltation of any ideology, party, or power above the authority of the Lord Jesus Christ.

We decree that every branch of government—executive, legislative, and judicial—is brought under divine order and accountability.

We decree that the fear of the Lord falls upon all leaders, judges, and legislators in this land.

We decree that righteousness and justice are reestablished as the foundation of national governance.

We prohibit corruption, bribery, deceit, and manipulation from holding influence in any office of authority.

We decree that every hidden work of darkness within governmental systems is exposed by the light of truth.

We deploy Angel Armies of revelation to uncover fraud, deceit, and unlawful alliances operating in secrecy.

We decree that honest elections and truthful representation are restored and preserved in perpetuity.

We prohibit interference, tampering, and deceit in the electoral process by foreign or domestic powers.

We decree that righteous men and women, filled with wisdom and integrity, are raised to seats of authority across every level of government.

We summon the Josephs, Daniels, and Esthers of this generation to govern in humility, courage, and righteousness.

We decree that unjust laws and unconstitutional mandates are struck down and rendered null and void in the courts of Heaven and on earth.

We prohibit the passage or enforcement of legislation contrary to the Word of God and the Bill of Rights.

We decree that the fear of man is broken off leaders, and that they govern in reverence to the Lord, not in compromise or intimidation.

We decree that divine counsel surrounds every righteous leader and silences the voice of corrupt advisors.

We decree that truth, transparency, and accountability are restored to every department, agency, and courtroom.

We prohibit censorship, surveillance, and unlawful control over citizens under the guise of safety or security.

We decree that the Constitution of the United States remains the law of the land, protected from manipulation, distortion, or overthrow.

We decree that Heaven's justice dismantles tyrannical systems, unlawful agendas, and ungodly alliances in government.

We decree that judges and lawmakers rule with equity, moral courage, and discernment from the Spirit of Truth.

We prohibit bloodshed, oppression, and exploitation carried out under the color of law.

We decree that the government of this nation shall once again serve the people, defend liberty, and uphold righteousness.

We decree revival fire into the hearts of public servants, awakening them to their divine assignment to steward justice.

We decree that the mountain of Government is reclaimed for Christ, established in truth, cleansed by fire, and aligned with the eternal government of His Kingdom.

We decree that the voice of wisdom cries out in every chamber and council, silencing confusion and establishing clarity of purpose.

We decree that divine order governs transitions of power, preventing chaos, deception, and the usurpation of lawful authority.

We decree that the spirit of truth rests upon all who draft, interpret, and execute law, ensuring alignment with justice and moral integrity.

We decree that America's covenant with liberty is renewed in righteousness, its foundations strengthened by repentance and divine mercy.

We decree that the breath of God sweeps through statehouses, courthouses, and city halls, cleansing atmospheres and dethroning pride.

We decree that angelic hosts guard the boundaries and gates of this nation, enforcing peace and repelling the counsel of wickedness.

We decree that the authority of the Cross stands as the supreme verdict over every governmental structure, judging deceit and vindicating righteousness.

We decree that divine strategies for national restoration are revealed to leaders who seek God's wisdom above human reasoning.

We decree that words spoken in deception or manipulation lose all power, while words of truth and life are established by Heaven's decree.

We decree that covenantal alliances among righteous statesmen and reformers are forged to restore justice and defend freedom.

We decree that governmental resources are stewarded with integrity, releasing provision to uplift communities and strengthen families.

We decree that a spirit of repentance sweeps through every level of leadership, replacing arrogance with humility and greed with service.

We decree that law enforcement and military institutions operate under divine protection, governed by honor, restraint, and courage.

We decree that peace reigns within America's borders, displacing violence, division, and terror with unity and safety.

We decree that truth in journalism and transparency in governance converge to illuminate darkness and protect the innocent.

We decree that every oath of office is remembered before Heaven, binding leaders to fulfill their duty under divine accountability.

We decree that the wisdom of Solomon and the discernment of Deborah rest upon judges and legislators who seek justice.

We decree that demonic thrones influencing policy are dismantled by the dominion of Christ's eternal government.

We decree that the counsel of the Lord establishes national security rooted in righteousness, not fear or domination.

We decree that the government of the United States stands as a testimony among nations—governed by truth, sustained by mercy, and overshadowed by the sovereignty of the Lamb.

IT IS SO ORDERED.

MEDIA MOUNTAIN

1. **Truth and Integrity in Communication**

   - Restoration of truth-telling, journalistic integrity, and factual reporting.
   - Exposure of propaganda, manipulation, and false narratives.

2. **Freedom of Speech and Press**

   - Protection of the constitutional right to free expression and dissent.
   - Defense against censorship, suppression, and monopolization of information.

3. **Sanctification of Digital and Social Platforms**

   - Purifying communication technologies from corruption and deception.
   - Reclaiming social media as a channel of truth, light, and prophetic voice.

4. **Protection from Psychological and Spiritual Manipulation**

   - Breaking the power of media sorcery, propaganda, and mind control.
   - Restoring discernment and critical thinking among the people.

5. **Righteous Storytelling and Cultural Influence**

- Raising up Kingdom storytellers, filmmakers, writers, and broadcasters.
- Replacing perversion and fear with hope, virtue, and truth.

6. Accountability of Media Corporations and Gatekeepers

- Exposing corruption, bribery, and collusion in news and tech industries.
- Ensuring media stewardship honors truth and serves the people, not agendas.

7. Global Witness of the Gospel through Media

- Reclaiming airwaves, platforms, and technologies for the advancement of the Kingdom.

- Declaring the Lordship of Christ over every sound, signal, and transmission.

AUTHORITIES FOR THE MEDIA MOUNTAIN DECREES

CONSTITUTIONAL AUTHORITY

- **First Amendment, U.S. Constitution (1791):**

"Congress shall make no law… abridging the freedom of speech, or of the press."

- **Declaration of Independence (1776):**

"That to secure these rights, Governments are instituted among Men."

- **Bill of Rights Preamble:**

Recognizing free communication of thought and opinion as essential to liberty.

BIBLICAL AUTHORITY

- *Proverbs 12:19 – "The truthful lip shall be established forever, but a lying tongue is but for a moment."*

- *John 8:32 – "You shall know the truth, and the truth shall make you free."*

- *Ephesians 4:25 – "Therefore, putting away lying, let each one of you speak truth with his neighbor."*

- *Psalm 68:11 – "The Lord gave the word; great was the company of those who proclaimed it."*

- *Matthew 10:27 – "What I tell you in the dark, speak in the light; and what you hear whispered, proclaim from the housetops."*

- *Luke 8:17 – "For nothing is hidden that will not be disclosed, nor is anything secret that will not become known."*

- *Psalm 19:4 – "Their sound has gone out to all the earth, and their words to the ends of the world."*

- *Revelation 14:6 – "Then I saw another angel flying in midair, and he had the eternal gospel to proclaim to those who live on the earth."*

PRAYER

Righteous Judge, Voice of Truth, and Author of all wisdom, we come before Your throne concerning the Mountain of Media. You are the God who speaks, and Your Word creates, convicts, and brings light into darkness. We acknowledge that communication was designed to transmit truth, not deception, and that words shape nations and destinies.

We present before You the constitutional guarantee of free speech and the biblical command to speak truth in love. We ask for verdicts from Heaven against lies, censorship, propaganda, and psychological warfare waged through media systems. Let every structure built upon deceit collapse under the weight of Your truth.

We appeal for the purification of airwaves, networks, and platforms, that they become channels of truth and revelation. Raise up righteous voices who will speak by the Spirit of Truth, and dethrone the powers of manipulation, fear, and corruption. Let the Gospel of the Kingdom be proclaimed through every medium to every nation until the earth is filled with the knowledge of Your glory.

In the name of Jesus Christ, the Word made flesh. So be it.

DECREES

We decree that the Spirit of Truth reigns over all forms of media in this nation and the nations of the earth.

We prohibit the spread of deception, propaganda, and manipulation through digital, print, or broadcast platforms.

We decree that journalistic integrity is restored and that truth becomes the highest standard in reporting.

We decree the exposure of lies, false narratives, and hidden agendas in every newsroom, newsroom boardroom, and algorithm.

We decree that censorship and suppression of truth are struck down and rendered powerless.

We prohibit media monopolies, information cartels, and collusion that silence righteous voices.

We decree that independent and righteous media rise with boldness to proclaim truth without fear.

We decree that whistleblowers, reformers, and truth-tellers uncover corruption and deception within communication systems.

We decree that social media platforms are cleansed of demonic influence, addiction, and manipulation.

We prohibit the use of artificial intelligence and data surveillance for censorship, propaganda, or control.

We decree that words of righteousness, faith, and justice flood the airwaves and transform national conversation.

We deploy Angel Armies assigned to truth to war against spirits of deception, slander, and perversion.

We decree that false prophets of media lose their platform, funding, and influence.

We prohibit the exaltation of fear, division, and confusion through news or entertainment outlets.

We decree that the light of truth exposes every hidden alliance between media, finance, and political corruption.

We release the Spirit of Wisdom to guide journalists, broadcasters, and creators into integrity and accountability.

We decree that righteous voices are amplified, protected, and given favor in every platform of influence.

We prohibit manipulation of children and youth through ungodly entertainment, advertising, or digital systems.

We decree that discernment increases among viewers and listeners, empowering them to reject deception.

We summon creative communicators, filmmakers, podcasters, and storytellers anointed to decree and declare truth and hope.

We decree that the Gospel of the Kingdom is broadcast freely and globally without censorship or restraint.

We prohibit foreign and domestic propaganda designed to undermine truth, faith, or freedom.

We decree that media giants bow to the authority of Christ and are reformed, divided, or replaced according to Heaven's justice.

We decree revival within media, networks, studios, and platforms shall be filled with light, truth, and redemption.

We decree that the Mountain of Media is reclaimed by the Lord Jesus Christ, purified by truth, governed by righteousness, and established as a voice of Heaven on earth.

We decree that the breath of the Almighty fills every medium of communication, transforming airwaves, digital streams, and written words into conduits of light.

We decree that the wisdom of Heaven overrides the counsel of darkness, compelling accuracy, fairness, and moral clarity in all reporting.

We decree that editors, producers, and executives are convicted by truth, compelled to choose integrity over influence and honesty over profit.

We decree that righteous storytelling overtakes sensationalism, producing content that uplifts, educates, and unites.

We decree that the veil of deceit is torn from the eyes of the public, and that nations awaken to discernment and moral courage.

We decree that angelic scribes record every righteous word spoken in truth, preserving testimony and silencing false witness.

We decree that media outlets devoted to righteousness receive supernatural favor, reach, and provision to expand their influence.

We decree that the algorithms and digital frameworks governing communication are recalibrated to promote truth and suppress corruption.

We decree that the spirit of fear loses its power to manipulate populations, replaced by messages of faith, hope, and reason.

We decree that divine justice is rendered against those who weaponize words to destroy reputations, nations, or faith.

We decree that every newsroom and studio becomes a place of accountability, where truth is honored as sacred trust.

We decree that righteous innovation emerges—platforms built on transparency and liberty that amplify truth across generations.

We decree that the voices of watchmen and prophetic communicators are strengthened, releasing warnings, guidance, and comfort to nations.

We decree that media education is purified, training future communicators to value accuracy, virtue, and discernment over popularity.

We decree that the sound of Heaven—the testimony of Jesus Christ—fills every medium until truth saturates the nations and the knowledge of the Lord covers the earth as the waters cover the sea.

IT IS SO ORDERED.

RELIGION MOUNTAIN

1. **Freedom of Worship**

   - Protection of the right to gather, pray, and worship God without government interference.
   - Safeguarding public and private expressions of faith.

2. **Freedom of Conscience & Belief**

   - Protection of the right to hold, change, or live according to one's faith convictions.
   - Defense against coercion into beliefs or practices contrary to conscience.

3. **Non-Establishment / No State Religion**

   - Prohibition of government creating or enforcing an official religion.
   - Protection against elevation of false religions or humanist ideologies as de facto "state religions."

4. **Free Exercise in the Public Square**

   - Ensuring believers can express and practice faith in schools, workplaces, government, and media.
   - Protection of faith-based organizations, ministries, and churches from discrimination.

5. **Freedom to Assemble for Worship & Ministry**

   - Right of churches, ministries, and believers to gather for worship, discipleship, evangelism, and fellowship.
   - Protection from unlawful shutdowns, harassment, or restrictions on assembly.

6. **Religious Liberty in Governance & Law**

    - No religious test for office (Article VI).

    - Ensuring elected officials can govern according to righteous conscience.

    - Defense against laws that would erode biblical morality under the guise of "neutrality."

7. **Global Spiritual Authority of Religious Freedom**

    - Recognition of religious liberty as a God-given right (not just a government-granted one).

    - Decrees that nations align with the principle of free worship of the true God, breaking the power of persecution.

AUTHORITIES FOR THE RELIGION MOUNTAIN DECREES

CONSTITUTIONAL AUTHORITY

- **First Amendment, U.S. Constitution (1791)**
  "Congress shall make no law respecting an establishment of religion, or prohibiting the free exercise thereof; or abridging the freedom of speech, or of the press; or the right of the people peaceably to assemble, and to petition the Government for a redress of grievances."

- **Article VI, Clause 3, U.S. Constitution**
  "No religious Test shall ever be required as a Qualification to any Office or public Trust under the United States."

BIBLICAL AUTHORITY

- *Job 22:28 – "You shall also decree a thing, and it shall be established for you; and light shall shine upon your ways."*

- *Psalm 22:27 – "All the ends of the world shall remember and turn to the Lord, and all the families of the nations shall worship before You."*

- *John 4:24 – "God is Spirit, and those who worship Him must worship in spirit and truth."*

- *Acts 5:29 – "We must obey God rather than men."*

- *Romans 14:5 – "Let each be fully convinced in his own mind."*

- *Galatians 5:1 – "Stand fast therefore in the liberty by which Christ has made us free, and do not be entangled again with a yoke of bondage."*

- *Hebrews 10:25 – "Not forsaking the assembling of ourselves together, as is the manner of some, but exhorting one another—and so much the more as you see the Day approaching."*

- *Matthew 18:20 – "For where two or three are gathered together in My name, I am there in the midst of them."*

- *Isaiah 33:22 – "For the Lord is our Judge, the Lord is our Lawgiver, the Lord is our King; He will save us."*

- *Amos 5:24 – "But let justice run down like water, and righteousness like a mighty stream."*

- *Isaiah 2:2 – "Now it shall come to pass in the latter days that the mountain of the Lord's house shall be established on the top of the mountains, and shall be exalted above the hills; and all nations shall flow to it."*

- *Revelation 11:15 – "The kingdoms of this world have become the kingdoms of our Lord and of His Christ, and He shall reign forever and ever!"*

- *Philippians 2:10–11 – "That at the name of Jesus every knee should bow, of those in heaven, and of those on earth, and of those under the earth, and that every tongue should confess that Jesus Christ is Lord, to the glory of God the Father."*

PRAYER

Righteous Judge of all the earth, we come before Your throne of grace and justice, acknowledging You as the Source of true liberty and the Sovereign over nations. We present as evidence the constitutional authority of the United States: *"Congress shall make no law respecting an establishment of religion, or prohibiting the free exercise thereof"* (First Amendment), and *"no religious Test shall ever be required as a Qualification to any Office or public Trust under the United States"* (Article VI). We also present the eternal witness of Your Word, which decrees: *"Where the Spirit of the Lord is, there is liberty"* (2 Corinthians 3:17) and *"We must obey God rather than men"* (Acts 5:29).

On this basis, we petition this Court for righteous verdicts in favor of religious liberty and worship of the true God. We ask for judgments against every principality, power, and earthly system that seeks to silence worship, coerce conscience, or enthrone false religions. Let the decrees issued from this Court establish unhindered worship, secure liberty of conscience, protect Your Ekklesia in assembly, and advance the Gospel throughout this land and the nations. We call for angelic enforcement of these verdicts and for the earth to align with Heaven's constitution in the mountain of Religion.

We ask all of these things in the mighty name of Christ Jesus, Our King. So be it.

DECREES

We decree that the worship of Almighty God shall not be prohibited, hindered, or silenced in this nation, but shall flow freely in public squares, private homes, churches, and assemblies, protected under both the Constitution and the decrees of Heaven.

We decree that every law, ordinance, or executive order that attempts to muzzle the praises of God's people is struck down in the Supreme Court of Heaven and rendered null, void, and unenforceable.

We decree that houses of worship shall be preserved, protected, and honored as sanctuaries for the presence of God.

We decree divine protection over every place of worship and prohibit acts of violence, harassment, or unlawful restriction from penetrating their walls. These sanctuaries are marked with the blood of Jesus and secured by angelic hosts.

We decree that true worshippers will arise in every city, lifting holy hands without wrath or doubting, releasing the fragrance of worship over this nation.

We decree that worship becomes a weapon of war, pulling down strongholds and enthroning the King of Glory in every gate.

We decree that a new sound of worship—louder than the voice of fear, division, or rebellion—will flood cities, homes, and government halls, shifting atmospheres, piercing deception, and driving back the powers of darkness. We enthrone Christ at the gates of culture, proclaiming Him Lord over this nation.

We decree that every individual in this nation shall be free to follow their conscience before God without coercion, intimidation, or penalty.

We decree that no government, institution, employer, or authority shall override or trample the God-given right of conscience, and every attempt to force allegiance to ungodly ideologies is struck down and rendered powerless.

We decree that no law, mandate, or policy shall compel the people of God to deny, alter, or compromise their faith in Christ, for Heaven's higher law overrules all unjust decrees.

We decree that manipulations of conscience through deception, propaganda, or indoctrination shall be exposed and rendered powerless, and that truth shall prevail over lies and coercion.

We decree that the Spirit of the Lord strengthens the resolve of believers to stand firm in their convictions, empowered to obey God rather than men.

We decree that courage, boldness, and steadfastness are imparted to the people of God, breaking all fear and compromise.

We decree that this land shall be known as a place where liberty of conscience is preserved, defended, and honored under both Heaven's authority and constitutional law, and that America's gates are shut to tyranny of conscience and open to the free worship of the true God.

We decree that no false religion, ideology, or humanist agenda shall be enthroned as the state religion of this land, and that the government shall not exalt or enforce any system of belief contrary to the worship of the Most High.

We decree that Christ alone is King, and His supremacy shall not be usurped by man-made systems.

We decree that every attempt to establish or elevate secularism, atheism, or idolatry as a ruling power in this land is struck down, and that all counterfeit thrones are dismantled, their decrees voided, and their structures dissolved.

We decree that no branch of government shall impose allegiance to a religious test, ideology, or doctrine as a condition for office, employment, or citizenship, and that righteous leaders shall not be silenced for their faith.

We decree that the mountain of Religion shall not be polluted by state control but remain free to exalt Christ above all, for He alone is Head of the Church and His Kingdom has no rival.

We decree that the banner of the Lord is lifted over this nation, and every counterfeit authority claiming divine allegiance is overruled, for the kingdoms of this world are becoming the kingdoms of our Lord and of His Christ.

We decree that the people of God shall freely proclaim the Gospel in schools, workplaces, government, media, and every sphere of society, and that no institution shall restrict or suppress the witness of Christ among the people.

We decree that faith-based organizations, ministries, and churches shall operate openly without fear of penalty or discrimination, and that their influence shall increase as their voices go forth unhindered.

We decree that righteous speech shall not be censored or criminalized under the guise of tolerance or neutrality, for truth is protected speech and will not be silenced.

We decree that believers shall walk in boldness and wisdom, releasing light in dark places and truth in deceptive systems, standing unashamed of the Gospel of Christ.

We decree that the freedom to live, speak, and act according to biblical conviction shall be preserved in every public setting until the knowledge of the Lord covers the earth as the waters cover the sea.

We decree that the assembling of the saints shall not be hindered, restricted, or dissolved by government, culture, or hostile powers.

We decree that the right to gather for worship, prayer, and fellowship is secured under Heaven's authority and constitutional law, and no force shall prevail against it.

We decree that every house of worship and ministry gathering is a sanctuary of the Lord, protected by the blood of Jesus and defended by angelic hosts.

We decree that any attempt to close, suppress, or regulate the gatherings of believers through unlawful mandates, intimidation, or persecution is void and carries no authority in this land.

We decree that the gatherings of the righteous shall multiply in homes, churches, stadiums, and public squares, releasing the presence, power, and government of God into the earth until revival covers the land.

We decree that no religious test shall ever be required for public office in this nation, and that men and women of faith shall not be disqualified or silenced for their allegiance to Christ.

We decree that righteousness exalts this nation through leaders who honor God, and that laws and policies contrary to His Word shall not stand in authority.

We decree that unjust statutes and unrighteous decrees are struck down in the courts of Heaven and lose enforcement on earth.

We decree that elected officials, judges, and lawmakers shall govern according to godly conscience, free from corruption and intimidation, their hearts aligned with truth and anchored in the fear of the Lord.

We decree that the foundation of law in this land shall reflect the eternal principles of God's Kingdom, and that Jesus Christ is recognized as the ultimate Lawgiver, Judge, and King.

We decree that nations shall open their gates to the worship of the true and living God, and that barriers, restrictions, and persecutions hindering the Gospel are broken.

We decree that the persecuted Church is strengthened, preserved, and delivered by the power of God, that imprisoned believers are released, and underground churches are protected.

We decree that every government and principality enforcing religious persecution is judged in the courts of Heaven, their decrees nullified, and their oppression overturned.

We decree that the freedom to worship Christ shall advance across borders, languages, and cultures until the knowledge of the Lord covers the earth as the waters cover the sea.

We decree that the kingdoms of this world are becoming the kingdoms of our Lord and of His Christ, and He shall reign forever and ever; every nation shall bow to His supremacy.

IT IS SO ORDERED.

ABOUT THE AUTHOR

Lisa Knight Windahl
1355 White Water Ln
Rockwall, TX 75087
lisa@verdictsandvictories.org

Lisa is a freelance paralegal who contracts with family law attorneys in the state of Texas. Lisa began her career as a paralegal in 1996, building a strong foundation in law and a deep commitment to justice. She is the proud mother of two grown sons and the grandmother of four, cherishing the joy and legacy of her family. Lisa's heart beats for serving the homeless and marginalized, bringing hope and tangible help to those in need. As a passionate follower of Christ, she is dedicated to equipping the Body of Christ with practical and spiritual tools to advance the Kingdom of God in the earth. Her life and work reflect a steadfast pursuit of righteousness, compassion, and Kingdom impact.

OTHER BOOKS BY THE AUTHOR

This is available at Amazon in Paperback, Kindle and Audible

Analyze & Execute is a strategic field manual that equips the Ekklesia to operate in high-level spiritual governance with precision, clarity, and authority. It lays out the foundational principles of jurisdiction, timing, standing, and alignment, training believers to discern Heaven's strategies and execute them with accuracy in the earth. Blending biblical revelation, legal reasoning, and practical instruction, this book teaches how to conduct proper spiritual intelligence assessments, identify legal ground, craft effective decrees, and wage war from a governmental posture. Used by intercessors, apostolic leaders, and prayer networks across the nation, **Analyze & Execute** continues to serve as a weapons-grade manual for those advancing the Kingdom of God in regions, systems, and nations.

Made in the USA
Coppell, TX
16 January 2026

69382814R00066